The
Mending
Ministry
of John

The Holy Word for Morning Revival

Witness Lee

Living Stream Ministry
Anaheim, CA • www.lsm.org

First Edition, December 2013.

ISBN 978-0-7363-6840-7

Published by

Living Stream Ministry
2431 W. La Palma Ave., Anaheim, CA 92801 U.S.A.
P. O. Box 2121, Anaheim, CA 92814 U.S.A.

Printed in the United States of America

13 14 15 / 4 3 2 1

2013 Thanksgiving Weekend Conference

THE MENDING MINISTRY OF JOHN

Contents

Preface

1. This book is intended as an aid to believers in developing a daily time of morning revival with the Lord in His word. At the same time, it provides a limited review of the Thanksgiving weekend conference held in Schaumburg, Illinois, November 28—December 1, 2013. The general subject of the conference was "The Mending Ministry of John." Through intimate contact with the Lord in His word, the believers can be constituted with life and truth and thereby equipped to prophesy in the meetings of the church unto the building up of the Body of Christ.

2. The book is divided into weeks. One conference message is covered per week. Each week presents first the message outline, followed by six daily portions, a hymn, and then some space for writing. The message outline has been divided into days, corresponding to the six daily portions. Each daily portion covers certain points and begins with a section entitled "Morning Nourishment." This section contains selected verses and a short reading that can provide rich spiritual nourishment through intimate fellowship with the Lord. The "Morning Nourishment" is followed by a section entitled "Today's Reading," a longer portion of ministry related to the day's main points. Each day's portion concludes with a short list of references for further reading and some space for the saints to make notes concerning their spiritual inspiration, enlightenment, and enjoyment to serve as a reminder of what they have received of the Lord that day.

3. The space provided at the end of each week is for composing a short prophecy. This prophecy can be composed by considering all of our daily notes, the "harvest" of our inspirations during the week, and preparing a main point with some sub-points to be spoken in the church meetings for the organic building up of the Body of Christ.

4. Following the last week in this volume, we have provided reading schedules for both the Old and New Testaments in the Recovery Version with footnotes. These schedules are

arranged so that one can read through both the Old and New Testaments of the Recovery Version with footnotes in two years.

5. As a practical aid to the saints' feeding on the Word throughout the day, we have provided verse cards at the end of the volume, which correspond to each day's Scripture reading. These may be cut out and carried along as a source of spiritual enlightenment and nourishment in the saints' daily lives.

6. The content of this book is taken primarily from the conference message outlines, the text and footnotes of the Recovery Version of the Bible, selections from the writings of Witness Lee and Watchman Nee, and *Hymns,* all of which are published by Living Stream Ministry.

7. The conference message outlines were compiled by Living Stream Ministry from the writings of Witness Lee and Watchman Nee. The outlines, footnotes, and cross-references in the Recovery Version of the Bible are by Witness Lee. Unless otherwise noted, the references cited in this publication are by Witness Lee.

8. For the sake of space, references to *The Collected Works of Watchman Nee* and *The Collected Works of Witness Lee* are abbreviated to *CWWN* and *CWWL,* respectively.

Thanksgiving Weekend Conference

(November 28—December 1, 2013)

General Subject:
The Mending Ministry of John

Banners:

The central requirement for the building up
of the church today is the mending ministry of life—
a ministry through which the broken spiritual net
is restored, perfected, and made stronger
and in which we experience Christ as our life
and become the dwelling place of God.

Christ is the good Shepherd who laid down His life
for the sheep so that, in the divine life,
there will be one flock and one Shepherd,
and now He is shepherding us in life
for the Father's house—
the divine and human incorporation
of the processed and consummated Triune God with
His redeemed, regenerated, and transformed elect.

Christ as the Son of Man is the High Priest,
clothed with a garment reaching to the feet
and girded about at the breasts with a golden girdle,
to cherish the churches in His humanity
and nourish them in His divinity.

While the Lord Jesus is arranging the world situation
so that God's people may go on,
He is also exercising His heavenly ministry
to especially supply God's lovers and seekers
with the heavenly riches, the divine element,
so that they may be kept at an overcoming level
and transformed into precious stones
for the building of God's dwelling place.

The Mending Ministry of Life

Scripture Reading: Matt. 4:21; John 21:11; 12:24; 1 John 1:1-2; 5:11-13, 16

Day 1   **I. The ministry of the apostle John was a mending ministry, a ministry of mending, or restoring, what had been damaged after the time of Paul's completing ministry; John mended the broken spiritual net, perfecting it and making it stronger (John 21:11; 1 John 1:1-2; 2:7-8):**

A. John's ministry was to mend the damage that had been done to Paul's completing ministry (2 Tim. 1:15).

B. After the death of Paul, Satan insidiously brought in heresies concerning the person of Christ and false teachings that damaged the church (1 John 2:18-19).

C. Because of the damage that had been done, there was the need for a mending ministry; John was mending what was damaged, and his writings repaired the torn fabric of the church (1:1-2; 2:20-25).

Day 2   **II. When the Lord appeared to James and John and called them, they were "mending their nets" (Matt. 4:21):**

A. The Greek word for *mending* in this verse is used in 1 Corinthians 1:10 ("attuned"), Galatians 6:1 ("restore"), Ephesians 4:12 ("perfecting"), and 1 Thessalonians 3:10 ("complete").

B. The mending ministry includes restoring, fixing, equipping, perfecting, completing, and framing together.

C. James and John were mending their nets not necessarily because they were broken; they were perfecting the nets, equipping them, and adding something to make the nets stronger and more complete.

D. The mending ministry is to fix, restore, perfect, prepare, complete, add to, adjust, equip, make suitable, and attune us so that we might be built up together with others (1 Cor. 1:10; 2 Cor. 13:9; Gal. 6:1; 1 Thes. 3:10).

E. Without the mending, a lot of materials may be brought into the church, but there will be no building; to pile material up requires no mending, but to build up that material requires much mending, perfecting, equipping, and attuning.

Day 3 **III. The ministry of the apostle John was a mending ministry of life (John 1:4; 10:10; 11:25; 1 John 1:1-2; 5:11-13, 16):**

A. The Gospel of John is a book of life (1:4; 3:15-16, 36; 5:24; 11:25; 14:6; 20:31):

1. The life John speaks of is the eternal, uncreated life; this life is actually the Triune God Himself (5:26; 11:25; 6:63).

2. The Lord Jesus came that we may have life abundantly; through His death and resurrection He released this life and imparted it into us (10:10; 12:24; 19:34; 20:17, 31).

B. This life is a wonderful person, indescribable in human language; when John referred to Him in 1 John 1:1, he could only say "that which was from the beginning," speaking of the One who was with the Father from eternity and was manifested to the apostles, who declared Him as life (vv. 2-3).

Day 4 C. Today's broken situation among the believers and in the churches can be mended only by the life-giving mending ministry; only life can mend (5:16):

1. There are "holes" in us and many broken things that need to be mended.

2. The holes and breaks must be mended by life in love; we can be mended only by the ministry of life (2:25; 3:16).

D. The central requirement for the building up of

the church today is the mending ministry of life;
it is in this ministry that we experience Christ
as our life and become the dwelling place of God
(John 2:19-22; 11:25; 14:2-3).

Day 5 **IV. In 1 John we see the basic and substantial
element of John's mending ministry (1:1-3, 7;
5:11-13):**
  A. The center of the revelation in 1 John is the
  divine fellowship of the divine life (1:3, 7):
    1. To enjoy the divine life, we need to abide in
    its fellowship according to the divine anoint-
    ing, based upon the divine birth with the
    divine seed for its development (2:12—3:10).
    2. By the terminating water, the redeeming
    blood, and the germinating Spirit, we have
    been born of God to be His children, pos-
    sessing His divine life and partaking of His
    divine nature (2:29—3:1; 5:1-13).
    3. Christ is now indwelling us through His
    Spirit to be our life and life supply so that
    we may grow with His divine element unto
    His likeness at His manifestation (3:1-2, 24;
    4:4, 14-15).
  B. To abide in the divine fellowship of the divine
  life is to enjoy the divine riches (2:6; 3:6):
    1. By such abiding, we walk in the divine light
    (1:5-7).
    2. By such abiding, we practice the truth, right-
    eousness, love, the will of God, and His com-
    mandments (v. 6; 2:5, 17, 29; 3:9-11; 4:7; 5:2).
  C. To preserve this abiding in the divine fellowship,
  three main negative things need to be dealt with—
  sin, the world, and idols (1:7, 9; 2:15-17; 5:21):
    1. The safeguard against these negative things
    is our divine birth with the divine life and the
    word of God that abides in us (v. 18; 2:14).
    2. In virtue of our divine birth, we also overcome
    Satan's evil world by our faith in the Son of
    God (5:4-5).

3. Our divine birth with the divine seed sown into our inner being enables us to not live habitually in sin (3:5, 9; 5:18).

4. In case we sin occasionally, we have our Paraclete as our propitiation to care for our case before our Father God, and the Son's everlasting, efficacious blood cleanses us (2:1-2; 1:7).

Day 6 V. **The revelation of Christ as the one grain producing many grains in His resurrection is overlooked by the vast majority of Christians (John 12:24):**

A. Christ as the one grain of wheat is the divine seed to produce many grains to be the many members of His organic Body, which consummates in the New Jerusalem (Rom. 12:3-4; Rev. 21:2, 10-11).

B. According to typology, the many grains are for the making of a loaf of bread; by the blending together of the grains into one loaf, the church as the Body of Christ was produced for His corporate expression (1 Cor. 10:17; 12:12, 27).

Morning Nourishment

1 John
1:1-2
That which was from the beginning, which we have heard, which we have seen with our eyes, which we beheld and our hands handled, concerning the Word of life (and the life was manifested, and we have seen and testify and report to you the eternal life, which was with the Father and was manifested to us).

John's ministry was a mending ministry. When Peter was called by the Lord, he was fishing, but when John was called, he was mending the net (Matt. 4:21). Peter did a great deal of fishing, bringing in a multitude of people. However, John mended the spiritual net, for his ministry of mending was a mending ministry of life. Only life can mend, covering all the holes in the spiritual net. How much this is needed today! There are so many holes in the Christian net. What can mend them? Nothing but life. This is the reason that we have been burdened over and over again with this matter of life. Some people laugh at us, saying, "Don't you know anything except the one word *life*?" Yes, in a sense, we only know life, nothing else. We do not know anything else because we do not need anything else. Life is our only need. (*Life-study of John,* p. 12)

Today's Reading

All of John's writings are the final words of the divine revelation in the Scriptures....Although many words may be spoken, the decision depends upon the final word. (*Life-study of John,* p. 12)

Paul's last book, 2 Timothy, was written about A.D. 66. During the next twenty-five years or so heresies sprang up, claiming that Christ was not God or that Christ had not come in the flesh. Thus, about A.D. 90 John's writings appeared. The Gospel of John was written to testify to the fact that Christ was indeed God (John 1:1; 20:28). His first Epistle was written to confirm that Christ had truly come in the flesh (1 John 4:2-3).

John's ministry, then, was to mend the damage which had been done to Paul's ministry. If the sleeve of my jacket gets

ripped, it must be mended according to the original pattern....
All it needs is to be made stronger where it was ripped; then it
is properly mended. The Lord's recovery today is in the time of
the mending ministry. We must therefore be brought back to
the original, but in a strengthened way.

How can we say that John's ministry is stronger than Paul's?
In other messages we have said that Paul's ministry is stronger
than John's! Now we are speaking from another standpoint.
Paul did tell us that the church is the Body of Christ, the fullness of the One who fills all in all, the household of God, the
house of God, the kingdom of God, the bride, and the warrior.
But Paul did not tell us that the church is a lampstand. Nor did
he tell us that the church will consummate in the New Jerusalem. Is a city not greater than a house? John's ministry is stronger, deeper, and higher than Paul's!

After the time of Paul, whose writings were finished about
A.D. 66, differing teachings crept in to damage the church. In
the quarter century after the death of Paul, Satan insidiously
brought in false teachings regarding both the Person of Christ
and the church. Heresies came in, claiming that Christ was not
God, was not the Son of God, and even that He did not come in
the flesh....Paul completed the revelation in the Bible, but
before too long it was damaged. Thus, after the completing
ministry, there needed to be a mending ministry. With these
two ministries the Bible is concluded. Notice that with John's
writings the Gospels are concluded; the Gospel of John was the
last to be written. Then his three Epistles are the conclusion of
the Epistles. Finally his Revelation brings to an end the New
Testament and even the whole Bible.

These writings were to repair the torn fabric of the church.
How much we owe to his mending ministry! (*The Mending
Ministry of John,* pp. 52, 2, 8)

Further Reading: Life-study of John, msg. 1; *The Mending Ministry of John,* ch. 1

Enlightenment and inspiration: _____

_____
_____
_____

Morning Nourishment

Matt. ...He saw another two brothers, James the *son* of
4:21 Zebedee and John his brother...mending their nets;
and He called them.
1 Cor. Now I beseech you, brothers, through the name of
1:10 our Lord Jesus Christ, that you all speak the same
thing and *that* there be no divisions among you,
but *that* you be attuned in the same mind and in
the same opinion.

When the Lord appeared to James and John, they were not
fishing, but mending their nets. The word *mending* is a good
translation, but it is not as good as the original text. This word is
the same as that used in Ephesians 4:12 for *perfecting* the
saints. Then in 1 Corinthians 1:10 this word is translated
"attuned," the only difference being that one is in the active voice
and the other in the passive.

In 1 Thessalonians 3:10 this word is translated "complete,"
that we may "complete the things that are lacking in your faith."
It would be correct to translate this verse in this way: that we
may "mend up the deficiencies in your faith."...Then Galatians
6:1 says, "Even if a man is overtaken in some offense, you who
are spiritual restore such a one in a spirit of meekness...."
Restore is the same word.

All of these different words have been used to translate this one
[Greek] word: *to prepare, to mend, to equip, to perfect, to complete,
to fix, to join together,* and *to restore.* (*CWWL, 1970,* vol. 1, p. 313)

Today's Reading

James and John were not necessarily mending their nets
because they were broken. They may have been broken, but it
does not mean exactly that. It means that they were fixing or
equipping their nets. They were adding something to the nets to
perfect them. They were perfecting the nets, equipping them,
and adding something to make the nets more complete.

The first kind of ministry is to fish for men—this means to

bring men into the kingdom of God. The second ministry is to mend men. The first ministry is to bring them in, and the second ministry is to build them up, to prepare them, to fix them, to equip them, and to make them more complete.

To follow the Lord is simply for these two ministries. The Lord Jesus called Peter and Andrew to participate in the fishing ministry. Then following this, the Lord called James and John to take care of the mending ministry. The fishing ministry is to bring people in, and the mending ministry is to fix, frame together, perfect, prepare, complete, add to, adjust, equip, make suitable, and attune in order that we all might be built up together with others. To follow Jesus is for these two ministries. We need to remember that these two ministries are outside of religion.

Without the mending, a lot of materials may be brought in, but there will be no building. Either the materials will be scattered, or they may be piled up. To be piled up is one thing, but to be built up is another. A heap of material is quite different from a building. To pile material up requires no mending, but to build up that material requires much mending, perfecting, equipping, and attuning. Therefore, in the church we need first the fishing ministry and then the mending ministry.

This is the way to follow the Lord Jesus in the New Testament service. It is not by working for Him that we follow Him. We need to be attracted by His shining, and we need to be transformed by His shining so that we become the light. Then we can be fishers and menders.

The New Jerusalem will be the ultimate issue of these two kinds of ministries. This is the Lord's intention, and this is what the Lord is doing today. It should be like this, and we need to be in this flow. We need to have the great light wrought into us so that we become the light, sharing either in the fishing ministry or in the mending ministry. (*CWWL, 1970,* vol.1, pp. 313-314, 318-319)

Further Reading: CWWL, 1970, vol. 1, "New Testament Service," ch. 9; *The Mending Ministry of John,* ch. 2

Enlightenment and inspiration: _____

_____
_____
_____

Morning Nourishment

John   In Him was life, and the life was the light of men.
1:4

10:10   The thief does not come except to steal and kill and
destroy; I have come that they may have life and
may have *it* abundantly.

11:25   ...I am the resurrection and the life; he who believes into Me, even if he should die, shall live.

Brothers and sisters, you need life. Other things may en-
large the holes; life will close every gap. We need John's ministry. John's ministry, the last ministry in the Bible and the
ministry with which the Bible concludes, was a mending ministry of life. (*Life-study of John,* p. 12)

Today's Reading

The Gospel of John is a book of life and it never gives
answers that are according to the tree of knowledge of good and
evil, but always turns people to the tree of life. There are no
answers of right or wrong, good or bad, yes or no. There is only
one thing—life. You do not need to be right, just like you do not
need to be wrong. You need only to care for life. When you have
life, everything is fine. (*Life-study of John,* p. 244)

Life is wonderful because it is mysterious. Even our human
life is a mystery. How much more the life of God! Life is mentioned repeatedly in the Gospel of John, far more than in the
other Gospels. The life John speaks of is the eternal, uncreated
life, which is God Himself. Surely such a life is a mystery! Eventually John tells us that this life is the divine Spirit Himself.

We can all be assured that this Christ is within us. Wherever we go, He is within. When we are happy with Him, attend-
ing the meetings, praying, and pray-reading, we may not have a
strong sense that He is within. But if we go against Him, He
will appear to us in a strong way. If we go to a movie or to a gam-
bling casino, He will speak to us from within, "What are you
doing here?" Our Lord is real, living, present, and within. We do
not have a religion. What need have we for a religion? We have

the living Christ! He is what we need and what we have.

John's mending ministry strongly stresses this point that Christ lives in us (14:17, 23; 15:4-5). He is real, living, and powerful, yet kind, loving, and patient. We must not think that if we offend Him, He will leave. The more we offend Him, the more He will convince us that He will never leave!

John first introduces Jesus as God. Eventually He tells us that this very One is now in us. He is the embodiment of the Father (14:8-11), He is the Son, and in resurrection He has become the indwelling Spirit. With Him we have the Triune God. He is our life.

The Gospel of John is a book of life. This life is simply the Triune God Himself. Christ came that we might have this life and might have it abundantly (John 10:10). Through His death and resurrection He released this life and has imparted it into us. We now have the Triune God within us as our life.

John [in 1 John 1:1-3] does not use the word *gospel*. Rather, what [the apostles] declared was life. He describes life as "that which was from the beginning," which they have heard, seen, and handled concerning the Word of life. This life, John says, was manifested and was seen by them; now they are declaring it to others.

What life is this? Was John presenting a doctrine? Was it the gospel? This life is a wonderful person, indescribable in human language. John could say only "that which" when he referred to Him! This person was with the Father from eternity. He was manifested and handled by the apostles, who then declared Him as life.

Surely it is a strange message which says that a person is life. In our natural thinking we do not consider life as a person. Life is one thing; a person is another. A person has life, but we do not say that he *is* life. John boldly declared—he does not say preached or taught—this life, who is a person. (*The Mending Ministry of John*, pp. 9, 16, 37, 53)

Further Reading: The Mending Ministry of John, chs. 3-5

Enlightenment and inspiration: _____

_____

_____

_____

Morning Nourishment

1 John If anyone sees his brother sinning a sin not unto
5:16 death, he shall ask and he will give life to him,
to those sinning not unto death. There is a sin unto
death; I do not say that he should make request
concerning that.

3:16 In this we know love, that He laid down His life on
our behalf, and we ought to lay down our lives
on behalf of the brothers.

[First John 5:16] is the only reference in the Bible to ministering life to someone. How is it possible to give life to someone?… I can give him, say, a watch, but what does it mean to give him life? It means that I impart Christ to him. It is of no help to talk doctrines to him. He has sinned because he is short of life. When we are short of the Lord Jesus, we commit sin. Doctrine will not help us to overcome sin. Only one person can overcome sin, and that is the Lord Jesus. (*The Mending Ministry of John,* p. 93)

Today's Reading

Husbands, do not rebuke your wife.…Rebuking makes the situation worse. What can you do? You may say that you must love her. Sometimes that may help, but love may corrupt and do damage. Only Christ works. Only life helps. We husbands must minister life to our wives.

Sisters, deep in your heart you may have the intention to subdue your husband. Husbands like to rebuke; wives like to subdue. You will never succeed in subduing your husband; God created man to be over you. The only husband who can be subdued is the clever one; he will merely be tricking you into thinking he is subdued. Give up your efforts to subdue your husband. What he needs is for you to minister life to him. You must minister a portion of Christ to him. Both husbands and wives need more Christ. Only He saves.

What short simple words John uses! "Give life to him"—a first grader can read this. Yet how marvelous is the expression, found nowhere else in the Bible! Some may protest that the Bible tells us to admonish and rebuke. It does, but this is not the word of the mending ministry here. Why is Christianity so degraded? One reason is that there are many to admonish but few to give life. What can mend today's broken situation? Only the life-giving mending ministry. (*The Mending Ministry of John,* pp. 93-94)

John's Gospel is not a book of teachings or gifts. In the Gospel of John and in Revelation as well, we do not see the teachings or the gifts; what we see is life. John's ministry was a ministry of the mending of life. There are many holes in us; there are many broken things, that need to be mended....Gifts bring in the breaks, divisions, in the Body. We can be mended only by the ministry of life.

First Corinthians speaks of the matter of divisions and shows that the cause of the divisions among the Corinthians was the gifts. In 1 Corinthians Paul says that the Corinthian believers did not lack in any gift (1:7). They had all the gifts, and because they paid too much attention to the gifts and overused the gifts, there were divisions among them. They needed the ministry of mending, and the apostle Paul ministered to them in this way. Chapter 13 of 1 Corinthians is the ministry of mending, the mending by love in life. The breaks and holes must be mended by love in life. Although we may speak in tongues and speak even the language of the angels, if we do not have love in life, we are like sounding brass, a sound without the life (v. 1). How different this is from being a branch in the vine or a grain of wheat, which quietly lives by Christ.

In a certain sense we do need teachings, and occasionally we need the gifts. But the central requirement for the building up of the church today is the mending ministry of life. It is in this ministry that we experience Christ as our life and as the tabernacle, the dwelling of God. By this ministry we will have the enlarged tabernacle as the very expression of Christ....By taking Christ as our life, we will all become a real, practical, living part of this greater tabernacle. (*The Vision of God's Building,* pp. 170-172)

Further Reading: The Mending Ministry of John, chs. 11-12; *CWWL, 1964,* vol. 4, "The Vision of God's Building," ch. 14

Enlightenment and inspiration: _____

_____

_____

_____

Morning Nourishment

1 John That which we have seen and heard we report also
1:3 to you that you also may have fellowship with us,
and indeed our fellowship is with the Father and
with His Son Jesus Christ.
7 But if we walk in the light as He is in the light, we
have fellowship with one another, and the blood of
Jesus His Son cleanses us from every sin.

The word *this* in 1 John 5:20 implies that God, Jesus Christ, and eternal life are one. In doctrine, there may be a distinction between God, Christ, and eternal life, but in our experience they are one. When we are in God and in Jesus Christ and when we experience eternal life, we find that all these are one. Therefore, John concludes verse 20 by saying, "This is the true God and eternal life." This sentence...is actually the conclusion of the entire book. What this Epistle reveals is the true God and eternal life.

John's last word, in 5:21, is the charge to guard ourselves from idols. Anything that is a substitute or replacement for the true God and eternal life is an idol. We need to live, walk, and have our being in this God and in this life. If we do not live in the true God and eternal life, then we shall have a substitute for the true God, and this substitute will be an idol. (*Life-study of 1 John,* pp. 356-357)

Today's Reading

The center of the revelation in 1 John is the divine fellowship of the divine life, the fellowship between the children of God and their Father God, who is not only the source of the divine life, but also light and love as the source of the enjoyment of the divine life (1:1-7). To enjoy the divine life we need to abide in its fellowship according to the divine anointing (2:12-28; 3:24), based upon the divine birth with the divine seed for its development (2:29—3:10). This divine birth was carried out by three means: the terminating water, the redeeming blood, and the germinating Spirit (5:1-13). By these we have been born of God to be His children, possessing His divine life and partaking of His divine nature (2:29—3:1). He is now indwelling us through His Spirit

(3:24; 4:4, 13) to be our life and life supply that we may grow with His divine element unto His likeness at His manifestation (3:1-2).

To abide in the divine fellowship of the divine life, that is, to abide in the Lord (2:6; 3:6), is to enjoy all His divine riches. By such abiding, we walk in the divine light (1:5-7) and practice the truth, righteousness, love, the will of God, and His commandments (1:6; 2:29, 5; 3:10-11; 2:17; 5:2) by the divine life received through the divine birth (2:29; 4:7).

To preserve this abiding in the divine fellowship, three main negative things need to be dealt with. The first is sin, which is lawlessness and unrighteousness (1:7—2:6; 3:4-10; 5:16-18). The second is the world, which is composed of the lust of the flesh, the lust of the eyes, and the vainglory of this life (2:15-17; 4:3-5; 5:4-5, 19). The last is idols, which are the heretical substitutes for the genuine God and the vain replacements of the real God (5:21). These three categories of exceedingly evil things are weapons used by the evil one, the devil, to frustrate, harm, and, if possible, even annihilate our abiding in the divine fellowship. The safeguard against his evil doing is our divine birth with the divine life (5:18), and, based upon the fact that the Son of God has through His death on the cross destroyed the works of the devil (3:8), we overcome him by the word of God that abides in us (2:14). In virtue of our divine birth, we also overcome his evil world by our faith in the Son of God (5:4-5). Moreover, our divine birth with the divine seed sown into our inner being enables us not to live habitually in sin (3:9; 5:18), because Christ has taken away sins through His death in the flesh (3:5). In case we sin occasionally, we have our Paraclete as our propitiation to care for our case before our Father God (2:1-2), and the Son's everlasting efficacious blood cleanses us (1:7). Such a revelation is the basic and substantial element of the apostle's mending ministry. (*Life-study of 1 John,* pp. 357-358)

Further Reading: Life-study of 1 John, msg. 40; *The Mending Ministry of John,* chs. 7-8

Enlightenment and inspiration: _____

_____

_____

_____

Morning Nourishment

John 12:24 Truly, truly, I say to you, Unless the grain of wheat falls into the ground and dies, it abides alone; but if it dies, it bears much fruit.

1 Cor. 10:17 Seeing that there is one bread, we who are many are one Body; for we all partake of the one bread.

In John 12:24 the Lord likened Himself to a grain of wheat.... Christ died in the form of a grain of wheat in order to release the divine life and impart it to us. Originally life is only in the single grain. But through death the life in this grain is released and imparted into many grains. We are those grains of wheat! (*The Mending Ministry of John,* p. 6)

Today's Reading

John 1:12-13 reveals that we are God's children. "But as many as received Him, to them He gave the authority to become children of God, to those who believe into His name, who were begotten not of blood, nor of the will of the flesh, nor of the will of man, but of God." How is it that we human beings can be children of God? It is because God's life has come into us. This came about because a grain of wheat fell into the ground and died. The life in that grain has been released into many grains. We are those many grains, God's children possessing His life.

What are the grains of wheat used for? They are to make a loaf of bread. We who are many are one bread, one Body (1 Cor. 10:17). The many sons of God are the members of Christ for Him to have a living Body.

This matter of the many grains possessing the divine life that Christ may have a Body is almost entirely overlooked by the vast majority of Christians. This item was damaged. John stepped in to repair the damage. The other Gospels do not cover this. It is John who tells us that our Christ was God; that He became a man to bring us reality and grace; that for us to receive Him He died on the cross—as the Lamb of God to take away our sins; as the brass serpent to destroy the devil; and as the grain of wheat to release the divine life into many grains, children of God for the Body of Christ.

From typology we know that the many grains are for the making of a loaf of bread. First Christ was alone, but after His death and resurrection many grains sprang up. By the blending together of these grains into one loaf, the church as the Body of Christ was produced. (*The Mending Ministry of John,* pp. 7-8, 41)

The Lord Jesus fell into the ground and died that His divine element, His divine life, might be released from within the shell of His humanity to produce many believers in resurrection (1 Pet. 1:3), just as a grain of wheat has its life element released by falling into the ground and growing up out of the ground to bear much fruit, that is, to bring forth many grains. Instead of receiving a warm welcome, the Lord preferred to fall into the ground and die as a grain of wheat that He might produce many grains for the church. The Lord, as a grain of wheat falling into the ground, lost His soul-life through death that He might release His eternal life in resurrection to the "many grains." (*Life-study of John,* p. 315)

Christ is the one grain of wheat (John 12:24) for death resulting in resurrection. This refers to Himself as the divine seed to produce many grains (the people who receive Him) to become His many members who constitute His organic Body which consummates in the New Jerusalem....Although we are the many grains, we do not like to be ground in order to be blended. But we need to be broken. Then we can be blended with others. We should not remain as whole grains. We have to be broken and ground into fine flour so that we can be blended with others for making a loaf. This loaf is the Body of Christ which consummates in the New Jerusalem. (*The Crystallization-study of the Gospel of John,* p. 83)

Further Reading: The Crystallization-study of the Gospel of John, msg. 7; *The Conclusion of the New Testament,* msg. 282; *Experiencing the Mingling of God with Man for the Oneness of the Body of Christ,* ch. 2

Enlightenment and inspiration: _____

_____

_____

_____

Hymns, #203

1   In the bosom of the Father,
         Ere the ages had begun,
    Thou wast in the Father's glory,
         God's unique begotten Son.
    When to us the Father gave Thee,
         Thou in person wast the same,
    All the fulness of the Father
         In the Spirit to proclaim.

2   By Thy death and resurrection,
         Thou wast made God's firstborn Son;
    By Thy life to us imparting,
         Was Thy duplication done.
    We, in Thee regenerated,
         Many sons to God became;
    Truly as Thy many brethren,
         We are as Thyself the same.

3   Once Thou wast the only grain, Lord,
         Falling to the earth to die,
    That thru death and resurrection
         Thou in life may multiply.
    We were brought forth in Thy nature
         And the many grains became;
    As one loaf we all are blended,
         All Thy fulness to proclaim.

4   We're Thy total reproduction,
         Thy dear Body and Thy Bride,
    Thine expression and Thy fulness,
         For Thee ever to abide.
    We are Thy continuation,
         Thy life-increase and Thy spread,
    Thy full growth and Thy rich surplus,
         One with Thee, our glorious Head.

Composition for prophecy with main point and sub-points: _____

_____

_____

_____

_____

_____

_____

_____

_____

_____

_____

_____

_____

_____

_____

_____

_____

_____

_____

_____

_____

_____

_____

_____

_____

_____

_____

_____

_____

_____

_____

_____

_____

The Revelation of the Triune God
and of the Consummated Spirit

Scripture Reading: John 1:1, 14, 29; 7:37-39; 14:7-20; 20:22

Day 1   **I. The Gospel of John reveals the Triune God—the Father as the source, the Son as the expression, and the Spirit as the realization (14:7-20):**

A. The Father is the source (6:46; 7:29; 13:3):
  1. No one has ever seen God the Father (1:18; 5:37; 6:46).
  2. All that the Father has is the Son's and is in the Son (16:15).
  3. The Father sent the Son (7:29; 6:57).
  4. The Father is expressed in the Son (14:7-11; 8:19).
  5. The Father is working in the Son (14:10; 7:16).

B. The Son is the expression (1:18):
  1. The Son is the Word who is God and who was with God in the beginning (v. 1).
  2. The Son is equal with God (5:18).
  3. The Son and the Father are one (10:30).
  4. The Son is the expression of the Father (14:8-9; 8:19).
  5. The Son lives because of the Father (6:57a).
  6. The Son came to carry out the Father's will (v. 38; 5:19-20, 30; 12:49).
  7. The Son became flesh, bringing grace and reality (1:14, 16-17; 8:32, 36).

Day 2
  8. The Son became a man to be the Lamb of God (1:29, 36).
  9. The Son baptized people in the Spirit (v. 33).
  10. The Son is life and the bread of life (11:25; 14:6; 6:35).
  11. The Son is a grain of wheat bearing much fruit (12:24).
  12. The Son is the good Shepherd who will gain

His flock (10:14-16).

13. The Son is the Bridegroom coming for His bride (3:29-30).

14. The Son is the vine cultivated by the Father (15:1).

15. The Son died, shedding His blood for the redemption of sins, and flowed out as living water, even as the Spirit (19:34; 7:38-39).

16. In resurrection the Son was breathed into us as the Spirit (20:22).

Day 3   C. The Spirit is the realization (14:17; 15:26; 16:13-15):

1. The Spirit is the reality of the Son (14:16-20; 15:26).

2. The Spirit receives all that the Son is and has obtained and discloses it to us (16:13-15).

3. The Father is in the Son, and the Son became the Spirit for us to drink so that He may become the living water flowing out of us (7:37-39; 4:10, 14).

4. The Spirit enters into us to be with us so that we may experience and enjoy the Son (14:17-18).

5. The Spirit being in us is the Son being in us (vv. 17, 20; 17:23, 26).

6. In the Spirit we are joined to the Triune God as one (vv. 21-23).

7. We worship God, who is Spirit, by this Spirit and with reality, that is, with the Christ whom we have experienced (4:23-24).

8. We are regenerated by the Spirit in our spirit, and we worship the Spirit in our spirit (3:6; 4:24).

Day 4 **II. The Gospel of John reveals the consummated Spirit as the consummation of the processed and consummated Triune God (7:39; 20:22):**

A. The consummated Spirit is the Triune God after He has passed through the process of incarnation, human living, crucifixion, and resurrection (7:39):

1. The process through which the Triune God passed to become the Spirit is an economical, not essential, matter (1:14; Heb. 9:14; 1 Cor. 15:45b):
    a. With God, change can never be essential; it can only be economical.
    b. In His economy God has changed in the sense of being processed; although God has changed in His economy, He has not changed in His essence.
2. *Processed* refers to the steps through which the Triune God has passed in the divine economy; *consummated* indicates that the process has been completed; and *the consummated Spirit* implies that the Spirit of God has been processed and has become the consummated Spirit (John 7:39).

Day 5

3. The Spirit of God was there from the beginning (Gen. 1:2), but the Spirit as "the Spirit of Christ" (Rom. 8:9), "the Spirit of Jesus Christ" (Phil. 1:19), was "not yet" at the time of John 7:39, because He was not yet glorified.
4. The Lord Jesus was glorified when He was resurrected, and through this glorification the Spirit of God became the Spirit of the incarnated, crucified, and resurrected Jesus Christ (Luke 24:26; Phil. 1:19).
5. The consummated Spirit is the compound of the Triune God, the man Jesus, His human living, His death, and His resurrection (John 7:39; Acts 16:7; Rom. 8:10-11; Phil. 1:19).

Day 6

B. The consummated Spirit was breathed as the holy breath into the disciples by the Son in resurrection (John 20:22):
    1. The Gospel of John reveals that Christ became flesh to be the Lamb of God and that in resurrection He became the life-giving Spirit; thus, in His resurrection He breathed

Himself as the consummated Spirit into the
disciples (1:29; 20:22):

a. The Holy Spirit in 20:22 is the Spirit expected in 7:39 and promised in 14:16-17,
26; 15:26; and 16:7-8, 13.

b. In resurrection Christ was transfigured
into the Spirit, and it is as the Spirit
that He was breathed into His disciples
so that He can live in the disciples and
they can live by Him and with Him and so
that He can abide in them and they can
abide in Him (20:22; 14:19-20; 15:4-5).

c. By breathing the Spirit into the disciples, the Lord Jesus imparted Himself
into them as life and everything.

d. The Holy Spirit in 20:22 is actually the
resurrected Christ Himself, because this
Spirit is His breath; the Spirit is the
breath of the Son.

e. The Lord is the Spirit who gives life, and
this Spirit is our breath.

2. The consummated Spirit as the breath is everything to us in living the Christian life;
only the breath, the Spirit, can be a Christian, and only the breath, the Spirit, can be
an overcomer (Gal. 3:2-3, 14; Phil. 1:19; Rev.
2:7).

Morning Nourishment

John **Not that anyone has seen the Father, except Him**
6:46 **who is from God, He has seen the Father.**
7:29 **I know Him, because I am from Him, and He sent Me.**
1:18 **No one has ever seen God; the only begotten Son, who is in the bosom of the Father, He has declared *Him*.**

Although the Bible reveals that God is one yet three, what is the biblical basis for saying that the Father is the source, the Son is the expression, and the Spirit is the realization? This conclusion is based on many years of studying the Bible in general and on studying the Gospel of John in particular. It is also based on comparing the Word with our own experiences. (*Taking Christ as Our Person for the Church Life*, p. 44)

Today's Reading

Concerning the Father as the source (John 6:46; 7:29; 13:3), we need to see five points. (1) No one has ever seen God the Father (1:18; 5:37; 6:46). (2) All that the Father has is the Son's (16:15), and all that the Father has is in the Son. The fullness of the Godhead dwells in Christ bodily (Col. 2:9). (3) The Father sent the Son (John 1:14; 7:29; 6:57). The Lord Jesus said many times that He was sent from the Father. The meaning of the word *from* in John 1:14 and 7:29 differs from our common understanding. Ordinarily, when we think of someone being sent, we think that the sender remains apart from the one being sent. However, the Greek word *para,* translated "from," means "by the side of," implying "with"; hence, it is, literally, "from with." This indicates that the Son was sent from the Father with the Father. When the Son came, the Father also came. The Son was sent by the Father, but the Father came with the Son and in the Son.

(4) The Father is expressed in the Son (14:7-11; 8:19). Hence, he who has seen the Son has seen the Father. (5) The Father is working in the Son (14:10; 7:16). The Father is expressed in the Son so that he who has seen the Son has seen the Father; moreover, the Father is working in the Son.

Concerning the Son as the expression (1:18), we need to see

the following [seven of] sixteen points. (1) The Son is the Word who is God and who was with God in the beginning (vv. 1-2). He is God, and He was with God. On one hand, verse 1 says, "The Word was with God," but on the other hand, it also says, "The Word was God." This is truly a mystery. (2) The Son is equal with God (5:18). (3) The Son and the Father are one (10:30; 17:22). The Father and the Son are equal, and They are also one. (4) The Son is the expression of the Father (14:8-9; 8:19). When the Son comes, the Father is expressed. (5) The Son lives because of the Father (6:57). The Son does not live apart from the Father. The Father and the Son, the Son and the Father, cannot be separated. (6) The Son came to carry out the Father's will (v. 38; 5:19-20, 30; 12:49). The Son did not do anything according to His own desire; He did everything according to the desire of the Father.

(7) The Son became flesh, bringing grace and reality (1:14, 16-17; 8:32, 36; 14:6). If the Son had not become flesh, both the Father and the Son would be too mysterious and abstract. The Son became flesh, passing from infancy through childhood into a man who was thirty years old when He began to minister. In the flesh God was expressed and made tangible to humanity. He was so tangible that He could even lie in a manger. Isaiah 9:6 says, "A child is born to us," and "A Son is given to us." The child was Jesus, but the Son who was given would be called Mighty God and Eternal Father. According to 1 John 1:2, the Word of life, who was with the Father, has been manifested, and we have seen, heard, and touched Him. John touched Him, Peter touched Him, and the other disciples touched Him.

When He became flesh, He brought grace and reality (John 1:14). Grace denotes enjoyment. The Son comes with God to be our enjoyment. At the same time, the Son comes also with reality. The incarnated Jesus is light, love, and life. He is the reality. (*Taking Christ as Our Person for the Church Life,* pp. 45-46)

Further Reading: The Economy of God and the Mystery of the Transmission of the Divine Trinity, chs. 4-5

Enlightenment and inspiration: _____

_____
_____
_____

Morning Nourishment

John **The next day he saw Jesus...and said, Behold, the**
1:29 **Lamb of God, who takes away the sin of the world!**
19:34 **But one of the soldiers pierced His side with a spear,**
and immediately there came out blood and water.

[Concerning the Son as the expression, we need to see two more of sixteen points:] (8) The Son became a man to be the Lamb of God to take away the sin of the world (John 1:29, 36). Not only did the Son become flesh, but He also became a man. As a man coming to be the Lamb of God, He had flesh and blood—a body. He bore our sins in His physical body, and He shed human blood to redeem us from our sins and to wash away our sins.

(9) The Son baptized people in the Spirit (v. 33). He not only took away the sin of the world but also baptized people in the Spirit. Sin was taken away, and the Spirit came. In the flesh through His incarnation the Son removed our sins, and in His resurrection He baptized us in the Spirit. (*Taking Christ as Our Person for the Church Life,* pp. 46-47)

Today's Reading

[We need to see the final seven of sixteen points concerning the Son as the expression:] (10) The Son is life so that people may have life; He is also the bread of life so that those who eat Him will live because of Him (John 14:6; 11:25; 10:10; 6:35, 57). He not only takes away our sins and baptizes us in the Spirit but also enters into us as life so that we may have life. He is also the bread of life as our life supply. Without Him as the bread of life, our life could not be sustained.

(11) The Son is a grain of wheat bearing much fruit (12:24). The Son as a grain of wheat fell into the ground and died. In His enlivening resurrection, He brought forth many grains. Today every one of us is one of the many grains; we all are grains produced by Him.

(12) The Son is the good Shepherd who will gain His flock (10:14-16). He is not only the grain of wheat that brings forth many grains but also the good Shepherd who cares for us. On

one hand, we are many grains, and on the other hand, we are many sheep as one flock. Today the Lord is shepherding us as His one flock.

(13) The Son is the Bridegroom coming for His bride (3:29-30). We are not only the many grains and the flock; we are also the bride waiting for the Bridegroom to come and marry us. On the one hand, we are already married to Him, but on the other hand, we are waiting for Him to come and marry us. He is the Bridegroom, and we are His bride.

(14) The Son is the vine cultivated by the Father (15:1). To cultivate is to carry out an economy. God the Father has a great economy in the universe, and this great economy is centered on the Son as the vine. We are the many branches of this vine (v. 5).

(15) The Son died, shedding His blood, for the redemption of sins and flowed out as living water, even as the Spirit (7:38-39; 19:34). The Lord took away our sins through the shedding of His blood in death, and He baptized us in the Spirit through the release of the Spirit, as living water, from within Him in resurrection.

(16) In resurrection the Son was breathed into us as the Spirit (20:22). All the foregoing fifteen points speak of what He is and has done. All these items are in the Spirit. He became the life-giving Spirit in resurrection, and He was breathed into us as the Spirit. In John 1:1 He is revealed as the Word who was with God and who was God, but at the end of the Gospel, He is revealed as the Spirit of life, the breath of life, to be breathed into us (20:22). Today the Lord is the Spirit. He is the last Adam who became the life-giving Spirit (1 Cor. 15:45). The last Adam, Jesus as the Lamb of God, accomplished redemption on the cross, and in His resurrection from the dead, He became the life-giving Spirit. When this life-giving Spirit is breathed into us, we receive the Spirit and life. (*Taking Christ as Our Person for the Church Life,* pp. 47-48)

Further Reading: The Economy of God and the Mystery of the Transmission of the Divine Trinity, ch. 6; *Crystallization-study of the Gospel of John,* msg. 3

Enlightenment and inspiration: _____

_____

_____

_____

Morning Nourishment

John   But when the Comforter comes, whom I will send to
15:26 you from the Father, the Spirit of reality, who pro-
**   ceeds from the Father, He will testify concerning Me.**
4:24   God is Spirit, and those who worship Him must
**   worship in spirit and truthfulness.**

In the Gospel of John, the Father is the source, the Son is the expression, and the Spirit is the realization. The Lord Jesus said, "I have come in the name of My Father" (5:43), and "the living Father has sent Me" (6:57; cf. 5:36-37). This proves that the Father is the source. The apostle John also says, "No one has ever seen God; the only begotten Son, who is in the bosom of the Father, He has declared Him" (1:18), and the Lord said, "He who has seen Me has seen the Father" (14:9). This shows that the Son is the expression. Later, the Lord also said, "I will ask the Father, and He will give you another Comforter, that He may be with you forever, even the Spirit of reality...because He abides with you and shall be in you" (vv. 16-17). Therefore, the Spirit is the reality, the realization, of God entering into us. From the standpoint of God's relationship with man, the Father as the source is expressed through the Son in order to be received as the Spirit. From the standpoint of man's relationship with God, as soon as we touch the Spirit, we receive the Triune God who enters into us. (*Taking Christ as Our Person for the Church Life,* pp. 44-45)

Today's Reading

Concerning the Spirit as the realization of God (John 14:17), we need to see the following eight points: (1) The Spirit is the reality of the Son (vv. 16-20; 15:26). All that the Father has is in the Son, and all that the Son has is realized as the Spirit. Apart from the Spirit, we cannot touch the Son. Hence, the Son is the Spirit, and the Spirit is the Son. When the Spirit comes, the Son also comes. When the Spirit is in us, the Son is also in us. All that the Father has is the Son's, and the Spirit receives everything from the Son. Today, the Spirit is in us for our experience and enjoyment.

(2) The Spirit receives all that the Son is and has obtained and discloses it to us (16:13-15). (3) The Father is in the Son, and the Son became the Spirit for us to drink so that He may become the living water flowing out of us (7:37-39; 4:10, 14). (4) The Spirit enters into us to be with us so that we may enjoy the Son (14:17-18). The One who is with us is the Spirit, yet the One whom we enjoy is the Son, because the Spirit is the Son. (5) The Spirit being in us is the Son being in us (vv. 17, 20; 17:23, 26).

(6) In the Spirit we are joined to the Triune God as one (vv. 21-23). In chapter 17 the Lord prayed to the Father, saying, "That they all may be one; even as You, Father, are in Me and I in You, that they also may be in Us...that they may be one, even as We are one; I in them, and You in Me, that they may be perfected into one" (vv. 21-23). This means that all those who believe into Him and have Him as life are joined as one in the Triune God and are joined to the Triune God as one. Hence, this oneness is not only horizontal but also vertical. It is horizontal because we, the many believers, are one; it is vertical because we, the many believers, are one with the Triune God. In the Spirit we are one with all the believers as well as with the Triune God.

(7) We worship God, who is Spirit, by this Spirit and with reality, that is, with the Christ whom we have experienced (4:23-24). Hence, we worship the Spirit by the Spirit. This is a mystery that cannot be explained.

(8) We are regenerated by the Spirit in our spirit, and we worship the Spirit in our spirit (3:6; 4:24).

These are the main points concerning the Father, the Son, and the Spirit in the Gospel of John. The Father, the Son, and the Spirit are the three-in-one God; He is one God, yet He is Father, Son, and Spirit. In His economy the Father is in the Son, the Son became the Spirit, and the Spirit enters into us. (*Taking Christ as Our Person for the Church Life,* pp. 48-49)

Further Reading: Taking Christ as Our Person for the Church Life, ch. 5; *Crystallization-study of the Gospel of John,* msg. 4

Enlightenment and inspiration: _____

_____
_____
_____

Morning Nourishment

John 7:39 But this He said concerning the Spirit, whom those who believed into Him were about to receive; for *the* Spirit was not yet, because Jesus had not yet been glorified.

1 Cor. 15:45 ...The last Adam *became* a life-giving Spirit.

In the Bible the Spirit is the consummation of the Triune God. However, this is not the Triune God apart from the process through which He has passed. The Spirit is the Triune God after He has passed through the process of incarnation, human living, crucifixion, resurrection, and ascension. Having passed through this process, the Triune God is now this consummate Spirit as the blessing of the New Testament. Thus, the Spirit is the blessing of God's New Testament economy. (*The Conclusion of the New Testament,* pp. 869-870)

Today's Reading

Before the incarnation, the Triune God was "raw," unprocessed. Through incarnation He was processed to become the last Adam. The Word, who is God, became flesh (John 1:1, 14)....In this process He was "baked" to become the bread of life (John 6:35). The point here is that whereas the Triune God was raw before incarnation, through incarnation He began to enter into a process.

After nine months in the virgin Mary's womb, the child who was the mighty God (Isa. 9:6) was born and placed in a manger (Luke 2:12)....For thirty years He lived in a carpenter's house. He Himself worked as a carpenter and was called a carpenter (Mark 6:3). Eventually He was crucified, being on the cross for six hours. He was buried and went to Hades, even descending into the lower parts of the earth (Eph. 4:9). Then He entered into resurrection, and in resurrection He, the last Adam, became the life-giving Spirit. All this was a process.

The process through which the Triune God passed to become the life-giving Spirit is an economical, not essential, matter. Change with God can only be economical; it can never be essential. Essentially, our God cannot change. From eternity to

eternity He remains the same in His essence. But in His economy the Triune God has changed in the sense of being processed. First, He who was merely God became a God-man. When
He was merely God, He did not have humanity. But when He
changed by becoming a God-man, humanity was added to His
divinity. This does not mean, however, that God changed in His
essence. On the contrary, He was changed only in His economy,
in His dispensation.

Although God has changed in His economy, no longer will He
change economically. Rather, He will remain the same. This is
the reason Hebrews 13:8 says, "Jesus Christ is the same yesterday and today, yes, even forever." Before "yesterday" Jesus
Christ did change economically. He changed by becoming a man.
He changed in resurrection by becoming the life-giving Spirit.
But now, after His resurrection, Jesus Christ remains the same.

Matthew 28:19 says "Go therefore and disciple all the nations,
baptizing them into the name of the Father and of the Son and of
the Holy Spirit." This charge was given by the Lord Jesus after
He had entered into resurrection, which was the consummation
of the process of the Triune God. The Triune God has passed
through a process that began with incarnation, included human
living and crucifixion, and consummated with resurrection. In
resurrection Christ, the embodiment of the Triune God, became
the life-giving Spirit. Now this Spirit is the consummation of the
Triune God for the believers to be baptized into the Divine Trinity.

The clearest revelation of the Divine Trinity is in Matthew
28:19. On the one hand, this verse speaks of the Father, the Son,
and the Holy Spirit; on the other hand, in this verse there is only
one name, the name of the Father and of the Son and of the Holy
Spirit. This is the completion of the process of the Triune God, a
process that ends in resurrection. (*The Conclusion of the New
Testament,* pp. 914-915, 1030-1031)

Further Reading: The Conclusion of the New Testament, msgs. 74,
80; *Crystallization-study of the Gospel of John,* msg. 8

Enlightenment and inspiration: _____

_____

_____

_____

Morning Nourishment

Luke 24:26   Was it not necessary for the Christ to suffer these things and enter into His glory?

Phil. 1:19   For I know that for me this will turn out to salvation through your petition and *the* bountiful supply of the Spirit of Jesus Christ.

Through the processes which the Triune God has completed, the Spirit of God as the processed Triune God has been consummated into the all-inclusive, life-giving Spirit.

He was consummated to be "the Spirit," who was not yet before the resurrection of Christ (John 7:39), compounded with Christ's divinity, humanity, death with its effectiveness, and resurrection with its power to be the compound anointing ointment (Exo. 30:23-25). The Spirit was not yet at the time of John 7:39 because He had not yet been consummated by the resurrection of Christ. Before the resurrection of Christ, that is, before Christ's glorification, the Spirit was not yet. The Spirit of God in the Old Testament was the Spirit with merely the divine element, but in resurrection He was compounded with the humanity of Christ, with His all-inclusive death and its effectiveness, and with His resurrection and its power, which repels all the negative things. He is now rich with all of these elements. (*Crystallization-study of the Gospel of John,* pp. 91-92)

Today's Reading

John 7:39 says, "But this He said concerning the Spirit, whom those who believed into Him were about to receive; for the Spirit was not yet, because Jesus had not yet been glorified." Many Christians do not understand the words *not yet* in this verse. The King James Version adds the word *given* in italics, showing that the translators were troubled by this verse. But verse 39 does not mean that the Spirit "was not given"; it means that the Spirit was "not yet." The Spirit was not there yet. The Spirit of God was there from the very beginning (Gen. 1:1-2), but the Spirit as "the Spirit of Christ" (Rom. 8:9), "the

Spirit of Jesus Christ" (Phil. 1:19), was "not yet" at the time the Lord Jesus spoke this word, because He was not yet glorified. Jesus was glorified when He was resurrected (Luke 24:26). After His resurrection, the Spirit of God became the Spirit of the incarnated, crucified, and resurrected Jesus Christ, who was breathed into the disciples by Christ in the evening of the day He was resurrected (John 20:22). The Spirit is now the "another Comforter,...the Spirit of reality" promised by Christ before His death (John 14:16-17). When the Spirit was the Spirit of God, He had only the divine element. When He became the Spirit of Jesus Christ through Christ's incarnation, crucifixion, and resurrection, He had both the divine and human element, with all the essence and reality of the incarnation, crucifixion, and resurrection of Christ. Hence, He is now the all-inclusive Spirit of Jesus Christ as the living water for us to receive. (*Life-study of John,* p. 219)

I hope that we all would receive a vision of *the* Spirit—He is the compound of the Triune God, the man Jesus, His human living, His death, and His resurrection. All the positive things in the universe are compounded in this one Spirit, which is *the* Spirit. The first four books of the New Testament are on the Son with the Father by the Spirit, but the next twenty-two books are on *the* Spirit, who is the compound of the Triune God, of the proper man, of the proper human living, of the death of Christ, and of the resurrection of Christ. This Spirit occupies twenty-two of the twenty-seven books of the New Testament. In the four Gospels it was the Son with the Father by the Spirit. Now it is the Spirit as the Son with the Father compounded with divinity, humanity, human living, death, and resurrection. The very Spirit who is in you today is such a Spirit. When we have this compound, all-inclusive, life-giving, processed Spirit, we have everything. This is for God's economy to dispense Himself into us. (*The Divine Economy,* pp. 76-77)

Further Reading: The Conclusion of the New Testament, msgs. 81, 85

Enlightenment and inspiration: _____

_____

_____

_____

Morning Nourishment

John **But when He, the Spirit of reality, comes, He will**
16:13 **guide you into all the reality; for He will not speak**
from Himself, but what He hears He will speak; and
He will declare to you the things that are coming.
20:22 **And when He had said this, He breathed into *them***
and said to them, Receive the Holy Spirit.

The resurrected Christ, the pneumatic Christ, was the Breather....The consummated Spirit is the divine breath, breathed by
the pneumatic Christ into the believers on the day of His resurrection. (*Crystallization-study of the Gospel of John,* p. 94)

Today's Reading

[The Spirit in John 20:22] was the Spirit expected in 7:39 and
promised in 14:16-17, 26; 15:26; and 16:7-8, 13. Hence, the Lord's
breathing of the Holy Spirit into the disciples was the fulfillment of His promise of the Holy Spirit as the Comforter....In
Acts 2 the Spirit as a rushing, violent wind came as power upon
the disciples for their work (Acts 1:8). Here [in John 20:22] the
Spirit as breath was breathed as life into the disciples for their
life. By breathing the Spirit into the disciples, the Lord imparted
Himself into them as life and everything.

As falling into the ground to die and growing out of the ground
transform the grain of wheat into another form, one that is new
and living, so the death and resurrection of the Lord transfigured Him from the flesh into the Spirit. As the last Adam in the
flesh, through the process of death and resurrection He became
a life-giving Spirit (1 Cor. 15:45). As He is the embodiment of the
Father, so the Spirit is the realization, the reality, of Him.

The Lord was the Word, and the Word is the eternal God
(John 1:1). For the accomplishing of God's eternal purpose, He
took two steps. First, He took the step of incarnation to become a
man in the flesh (1:14), to be the Lamb of God to accomplish
redemption for man (1:29), to declare God to man (1:18), and to
manifest the Father to His believers (14:9-11). Second, He took
the step of death and resurrection to be transfigured into the

Spirit that He might impart Himself into His believers as their life and their everything, and that He might bring forth many sons of God, His many brothers, for the building of His Body, the church, the habitation of God, to express the Triune God for eternity. Hence, originally He was the eternal Word; then, through His incarnation He became flesh to accomplish God's redemption, and through His death and resurrection He became the Spirit to be everything and do everything for the completion of God's building. (John 20:22, footnote 1)

The Lord Jesus then breathed into the disciples, and He asked the disciples to receive that breath. He called that breath the Holy Spirit....The Holy Spirit is the breath of the Son. We cannot say that the breath is one person, and the breather is another person. These verses show us clearly that the Spirit is not another person, but the very breath of the Son. We should not consider that the breather is a person and the breath is another person. Actually, the breath is one person with the breather. The resurrected Christ as the life-giving Spirit is the breath. (*God's New Testament Economy,* p. 80)

Second Corinthians 3:6 says, "The letter kills, but the Spirit gives life."...Verse 17 declares, "And the Lord is the Spirit." The Lord is the Spirit who gives life, and this Spirit is our breath. (*Life-study of Philippians,* p. 300)

To be a Christian is not merely difficult—it is impossible. Only the processed and consummated Triune God living in us as the all-inclusive Spirit can be a Christian. What the New Testament requires of us is too high. The kind of holiness required, for example, is something that we cannot produce. We praise the Lord that it is not we who need to fulfill the New Testament requirements but the Spirit in us who fulfills them. Instead of doing things in ourselves, we should simply enjoy His living and His working. Only the Spirit can be a Christian, and only the Spirit can be an overcomer. (*Life-study of Job,* p. 109)

Further Reading: Life-study of John, msgs. 46-47

Enlightenment and inspiration: _____

_____

_____

_____

Hymns, #1114

1   The Spirit today is the air that we breathe;
Our spirits rejoice in this living inflow.
For just as our body the breath does receive,
So also in spirit to live it is so.

2   The Spirit today is the air that we breathe;
What thing more important than breathing to do?
For breathing each moment, new life we receive,
And God's living freshness is constant and new.

3   For God has been processed, as air now, He's free;
This life-giving pneuma is all that we need.
He's rich and abundant, so plentiful, He,
In spirit to walk is to breathe Him indeed.

4   O, say, aren't you glad that the Spirit's outpoured
And God, fully processed, is flowing in us?
So freely we're breathing this life-giving Lord,
And breathing, receiving His life, glorious!

Composition for prophecy with main point and sub-points: _____

_____

_____

_____

_____

_____

_____

_____

_____

_____

_____

_____

_____

_____

_____

_____

_____

_____

_____

_____

_____

_____

_____

_____

_____

_____

_____

_____

_____

_____

_____

_____

_____

_____

_____

_____

_____

The Shepherding of Christ
for the Church
as the One Flock and the Father's House

Scripture Reading: John 10:10-11, 15-17; 14:2-3

Day 1 I. According to the Gospel of John, the Triune
God as life brings forth the church; although
the word *church* is not used, many verses
allude to the church (2:16-22; 3:26-30; 10:16;
11:52; 12:24; 14:2-3; 15:5; 17:11, 21-23).

II. Christ is the good Shepherd who laid down
His life for the sheep so that, in the divine
life, there will be one flock and one Shepherd
(10:16):

A. As the good Shepherd, the Lord Jesus came that we
might have life and have it abundantly (vv. 10-11).

B. The good Shepherd laid down His human life to
accomplish redemption for His sheep that they
may share His divine life (vv. 11, 15, 17).

Day 2 C. As the good Shepherd, the Lord shepherds us by
feeding us with Himself and in Himself as the
pasture (v. 9):

1. The work of shepherding is the work of
feeding (Matt. 9:36; 14:14-21).

2. The pasture signifies Christ as the feeding
place of the sheep (John 10:9):

a. Today our pasture is the resurrected
Christ as the life-giving Spirit (11:25;
1 Cor. 15:45b).

b. In our daily Christian life we should have
the sense that we are in the pasture enjoying Christ as the rich supply of life.

D. As the good Shepherd, the Lord is leading, guiding, and directing us in the divine life (John
10:14, 27-30):

1. The Lord shepherds us in life from within:

a. Inwardly we have Him as our Shepherd,
a Shepherd of life and in life (v. 10).

      b. As our Shepherd, the living Christ not only gives us life—He is our life (v. 10; 11:25; 14:6; Col. 3:4).

  2. Christ shepherds us by being life to us and by living in us; His living within us is actually His shepherding.

E. Under the shepherding of Christ as the good Shepherd, "there shall be one flock, one Shepherd" (John 10:16):

  1. The one flock signifies the one church, the one Body of Christ, brought forth by the Lord's eternal, divine life, which He imparted into His members through His death (vv. 16-18; Eph. 2:14-16; 3:6).

Day 3

  2. The Lord has formed the Jewish believers and the Gentile believers into one flock—the one church, the Body of Christ—under His shepherding (John 10:10-18; Eph. 2:14-16; 3:6).

  3. The Lord's sheep have received the divine life, and by the divine life the sheep live together as one flock.

  4. As the good Shepherd, the Lord causes us to flock together (John 10:16; Luke 12:32; Acts 20:28; 1 Pet. 5:2-3; cf. Isa. 40:11).

F. John 21, a chapter on shepherding, is the completion and consummation of the Gospel of John; shepherding is the key to the Gospel of John:

  1. If we do not know what shepherding is, the entire Gospel of John will be in vain to us; it is only when we shepherd others that we can know John in an intrinsic way (3:16; 4:10, 14; 10:9-18; 21:15-17).

  2. The Gospel of John is a book on Christ coming to be our life by cherishing and nourishing us; to cherish others is to make them happy, pleasant, and comfortable (Matt. 9:10; Luke 7:34), and to nourish others is to feed them with the all-inclusive Christ (Matt. 24:45-47).

3. After His resurrection the Lord incorpo-
rated the apostolic ministry with His heavenly ministry to take care of God's flock, the
church, which issues in the Body of Christ
(John 21:15-17).

Day 4 III. **The Lord Jesus is shepherding us in life for**
the Father's house—the divine and human
incorporation of the processed and consum-
mated Triune God with His redeemed, re-
generated, and transformed elect (14:2-3):

A. We need to see life and building as revealed in
the Gospel of John:

1. Life is for building, and the building is of
life (11:25; 14:2).

2. The Gospel of John reveals that the Triune
God is dispensing Himself as life into His
believers and that the believers, as the result
of this dispensing, become the building of
God, His expansion, enlargement, and corporate expression (1:4; 10:10b; 11:25; 14:2-3, 6).

Day 5 B. In His resurrection the Lord Jesus rebuilt God's
temple in a larger way, making it a corporate
one, the mystical Body of Christ (2:19-22):

1. The body of Jesus, the temple, that was
destroyed on the cross was small and weak,
but the Body of Christ in resurrection
is vast and powerful (1 Cor. 3:16-17; Eph.
1:22-23).

2. Since the day of His resurrection, the Lord
Jesus has been enlarging His Body in resurrection life; He is still working for the
building of His Body under the process of
resurrection (John 2:19-22).

3. Christ, who is the resurrection and the life
(11:25), changes death into life for the building of the house of God; our living as Christians is a life of changing death into life for
the building up of the mystical Body of
Christ (2:1-21).

C. The Father's house is a matter of the Triune God, through incarnation, crucifixion, and resurrection, working Himself into the believers in order to be fully mingled with them so that He may build them up as an organism for His dwelling and expression (14:2-3, 23):

1. The Lord's coming brought God into man, and His going brought man into God; by this coming and going, He builds up the house of God by building God into man and man into God (1:14; 10:10b; 14:2-3).

2. By the Spirit and through His death and resurrection, the Son of God, the Lord Jesus Christ, is building an organism, the church, which is His Body and the Father's house, produced by the mingling of the Triune God with His chosen and redeemed people (vv. 7-24).

3. The Father's house is in three stages: the stage of God incarnate, the stage of Christ resurrected with His believers to be built up as the church, and the consummate stage— the New Jerusalem (2:19-21; Rev. 21:2-3, 9-10).

Morning Nourishment

John 10:10-11	The thief does not come except to steal and kill and destroy; I have come that they may have life and may have *it* abundantly. I am the good Shepherd; the good Shepherd lays down His life for the sheep.
15	Even as the Father knows Me and I know the Father; and I lay down My life for the sheep.

The Gospel of John is a book of life. This life is simply the Triune God Himself....Life always has an issue. Living things bring forth fruit. Surely the divine life will have a divine result. In the Gospel of John the Triune God as the divine life brings forth the church. Though this actual term is not used in John, the implication is strongly apparent. (*The Mending Ministry of John,* p. 37)

Today's Reading

[In John 10] the good Shepherd is Christ, who laid down His *psuche* life for His sheep so that they may have the *zoe* life and may have it abundantly (vv. 2, 10-11, 14-15, 17-18). In 10:11 the Lord Jesus said concerning Himself, "I am the good Shepherd; the good Shepherd lays down His life for the sheep." In verse 14 the Lord went on to say, "I am the good Shepherd, and I know My own, and My own know Me." As the good Shepherd, the Lord laid down His life on behalf of the sheep. Today the Lord is still our Shepherd. (*The Fulfillment of the Tabernacle and the Offerings in the Writings of John,* p. 255)

[In John 10:10 and 11] two different Greek words are used for *life.* In verse 10 the Greek word is *zoe,* which is the word used in the New Testament for the eternal divine life. In verse 11 the Greek word is *psuche,* the same word for *soul,* which means the soulish life, that is, the human life. These two verses indicate that the Lord Jesus has two kinds of lives. As a man the Lord has the *psuche* life, the human life, and as God He has the *zoe* life, the divine life.

The Lord's divine life could never be slain. What was slain in His crucifixion was His human life. In order to be our Savior, He, as a man, laid down His human life to accomplish redemption for us that we might receive His *zoe* life. He laid down His human life in order that we, after being redeemed, might receive His *zoe* life, the eternal life.

In the divine life we are all one entity, meaning that we are one flock under one Shepherd in one life....A sheep is a regenerated person with the divine life. We all must live by the divine life and thus become genuine, real, and pure sheep. Then we shall all be in the flock....The flock is produced, kept, maintained, and formed by the divine life. How good it is for brethren to dwell together in unity (Psa. 133:1). However, dwelling in unity simply means to dwell in the divine life. Praise the Lord that in the divine life we are truly one and love one another. This is not possible in our human, *psuche* life, but only in the divine, *zoe* life. We receive this *zoe* life through the redemption accomplished by our Shepherd who laid down His *psuche* life. He sacrificed His *psuche* life to accomplish redemption for us all that we might receive Him as our *zoe* life. Now we are in the *zoe* life under one Shepherd to be one flock. This is not an organization; it is a flocking together in life. It is wonderful. Hallelujah! (*Life-study of John,* pp. 265-267)

Christ is our door, our Shepherd, and our pasture. As the door, He is our freedom, and as the Shepherd, He is leading, guiding, and directing us in life....As the pasture Christ is our life supply. Day by day, we need to enjoy Christ as our pasture. (*The Fulfillment of the Tabernacle and the Offerings in the Writings of John,* p. 257)

We are nothing and nobodies, but we are feeders of the sheep for God. I find it difficult to answer people when they ask me about my profession. A number of times I have replied, "It is hard for me to say. In a sense I am nobody. In another sense I am wonderful." On the one hand I am nobody, vanity; on the other hand I am a wonderful person doing the wonderful job of feeding the sheep for God. Nothing is more wonderful than the work of feeding the sheep for God. (*Life-study of Genesis,* p. 292)

Further Reading: The Fulfillment of the Tabernacle and the Offerings in the Writings of John, chs. 27-28

Enlightenment and inspiration: _____

_____
_____
_____

Morning Nourishment

John **I am the door; if anyone enters through Me, he**
10:9 **shall be saved and shall go in and go out and shall**
find pasture.
Matt. **And seeing the crowds, He was moved with com-**
9:36 **passion for them, because they were harassed and**
cast away like sheep not having a shepherd.

The Shepherd, who is life to us, leads us, guides us, and
directs us in everything. Therefore, we should not be directed
by anything outward but instead should be directed inwardly
by Christ who is life to us. This Christ is our Shepherd, our
Guide. (*The Fulfillment of the Tabernacle and the Offerings in
the Writings of John,* p. 257)

Today's Reading

The pasture [in John 10:9] signifies Christ as the feeding place
for the sheep. When the pasture is not available in the wintertime
or in the night, the sheep must be kept in the fold. When the pasture is ready, there is no further need for the sheep to remain in
the fold. To be kept in the fold is transitory and temporary. To be in
the pasture to enjoy its riches is final and permanent. Before
Christ came, the law was a ward, and to be under the law was
transitory. Now, since Christ has come, all God's chosen people
must come out of the law and come into Him to enjoy Him as their
pasture (Gal. 3:23-25; 4:3-5). This should be final and permanent.

The pasture is a place full of tender grass; that is, a pasture is
a place full of the supply of life....Today our pasture is the resurrected Christ as the life-giving Spirit. In our daily Christian life
we need to have the definite realization that we are in the pasture enjoying Christ as the rich supply of life. (*The Fulfillment of
the Tabernacle and the Offerings in the Writings of John,* p. 257)

Psalm 23:1 says, "Jehovah is my Shepherd." The main thing
a shepherd does is to feed the sheep. In John 10:11 the Lord
Jesus said, "I am the good Shepherd; the good Shepherd lays
down His life for the sheep." As a man the Lord Jesus has the
human life, and as God He has the divine life. The Lord laid

down His human life to accomplish redemption for His sheep (John 10:15, 17-18) so that they may have His divine life (John 10:10), the eternal life (John 10:28), by which they may be formed into one flock under Himself as the one Shepherd. As the good Shepherd, Christ feeds His sheep with the divine life in this way and for this purpose.

Christ is our Shepherd, and we are His sheep. Now the Lord shepherds us in life from within. Inwardly we have Him as our Shepherd, a Shepherd of life and in life. As our Shepherd, the living Christ not only gives us life—He is life to us. The living of the Lord within us is actually His shepherding. Christ shepherds us by being life to us and by living in us. (*The Conclusion of the New Testament,* pp. 474-475)

It is important for us to realize that the Lord shepherds us not in the way of outward activity, but...inwardly in the way of life. This means that the Lord shepherds us from within. Inwardly, we have Him as our Shepherd, as a Shepherd of life and in life. How does the Lord Jesus shepherd us? He shepherds us in life.

The Lord first called and brought His Jewish believers out of the fold of the Jewish religion, and after Pentecost He saved and brought many Gentile believers out of the Gentile world to make them all, both the Jewish believers and the Gentile believers, one flock under Himself as the one Shepherd (John 10:16b). This one flock is the one, universal church, the one Body of Christ (Eph. 2:14-16; 3:6). It no longer belongs to the Jewish fold or to the Gentile world but stands by itself as the church of Christ set apart from the Jews and the Gentiles (1 Cor. 10:32). (*The Fulfillment of the Tabernacle and the Offerings in the Writings of John,* pp. 255, 258)

The one flock [in John 10:16] signifies the one church, the one Body of Christ (Eph. 2:14-16; 3:6), brought forth by the Lord's eternal, divine life, which He imparted into His members through His death (John 10:10-18). (John 10:16, footnote 2)

Further Reading: Life-study of John, msg. 22; *Crystallization-study of the Gospel of John,* msg. 7

Enlightenment and inspiration: _____

_____

_____

_____

Morning Nourishment

John
10:16   And I have other sheep, which are not of this fold; I must lead them also, and they shall hear My voice, and there shall be one flock, one Shepherd.

21:16   ...Simon, *son* of John, do you love Me? He said to Him, Yes, Lord, You know that I love You. He said to him, Shepherd My sheep.

The flock is the church which includes two peoples—the believing Jews and Gentiles. The Lord brings both together into one flock and under one Shepherd. Now, the one flock and the one Shepherd are the one Body and the one Head.

Why are the Shepherd, the divine life, and the human life all for the flock? Because the people in the flock are fallen persons in need of redemption. As a man, the Shepherd had the human life. He sacrificed His human life in order to accomplish redemption for His flock. In this way His flock was redeemed. Then His flock received His divine life, and by this divine life the sheep live together as the flock. Thus, the flock is formed into one unit, into one entity. This is not accomplished by the human life, but by the divine life. (*Life-study of John,* p. 266)

Today's Reading

The more we enjoy the life of Christ, the more we desire to be with the flock. If we have no interest in the life and no growth in life, we do not care about the church life. But when we receive life from Christ and that life grows in us so that we enjoy life more abundant, there wells up within us the desire for the church life. We feel like scattered sheep, and our longing is to be gathered together into one flock. Thus, John 10, a chapter on life, alludes to the church, the one flock. (*The Mending Ministry of John,* p. 40)

John 21 is a chapter on shepherding....This chapter is not merely an appendix but also the completion and consummation of the Gospel of John, a book on Christ being God coming to be our life. The writer of this Gospel spent twenty chapters to unveil such a Christ. Eventually, such a book has a conclusion on shepherding. If we do not know what shepherding is, the entire

Gospel of John will be in vain to us. It is only when we shepherd others that we can know John in an intrinsic way. Shepherding is the key to the Gospel of John.... [In John 21:15] Peter said, "Lord, You know," because he had denied the Lord three times. He lost his natural confidence in his love toward the Lord. In restoring Peter's love toward Him, the Lord charged him to shepherd and feed His sheep....Without shepherding, there is no way for us to minister life to others. John is the Gospel of life. If we want to enjoy life and minister life to others, we must shepherd them.

To cherish people is to make them happy and to make them feel pleasant and comfortable. We must have a pleasant countenance when we contact people. We should be happy and rejoicing. We should not contact anyone with a cheerless countenance. We must give people the impression that we are genuinely happy and pleasant. Otherwise, we will not be able to cherish them, to make them happy. Then we should go on to nourish them. We do not nourish people when we speak to them about marriage, courtship, politics, the world situation, or education. To nourish people is to feed them with the all-inclusive Christ.

In order to nourish people with Christ, we first have to seek Christ, experience Christ, gain Christ, enjoy Christ, and participate in Christ. (*The Vital Groups,* pp. 60-61, 102-103)

When the Lord stayed with His disciples after His resurrection and before His ascension, in one of His appearings, He commissioned Peter to feed His lambs and shepherd His sheep in His absence, while He is in the heavens (John 21:15-17). Shepherding implies feeding, but it includes much more than feeding. To shepherd is to take all-inclusive tender care of the flock.... This is to incorporate the apostolic ministry with Christ's heavenly ministry to take care of God's flock, which is the church that issues in the Body of Christ. (*Crystallization-study of the Gospel of John,* p. 131)

Further Reading: The Mending Ministry of John, ch. 5; The Vital Groups, msgs. 7, 11

Enlightenment and inspiration: _____

_____
_____
_____

Morning Nourishment

John Jesus said..., I am the resurrection and the life; he
11:25 who believes into Me, even if he should die, shall live.
14:2 In My Father's house are many abodes; if *it were*
not *so,* I would have told you; for I go to prepare a
place for you.

The Father's house is a divine and human incorporation of the
processed and consummated God constituted with His redeemed,
regenerated, and transformed elect. The Father's house is not
only a constitution—it is an incorporation. (*The Issue of Christ
Being Glorified by the Father with the Divine Glory,* p. 32)

Today's Reading

Many times in the past we have stressed that the Bible covers
two main matters—Christ and the church. However, considered
from another angle, the Bible is a book of life and building. Christ
is life [Col. 3:4], and the church is a building....If you fail to realize
that Christ is life and that the church is a building, then when you
say these words they will simply be doctrinal terms.

The Bible is very consistent. If you read it with insight and
with the heavenly vision, you will discover that it begins with life
and building. We see life and building in Genesis 2. Immediately
after the creation of man, life was introduced. After the Lord God
created man, He placed him in a garden in front of the tree of life
(Gen. 2:7-9). Following this mention of the tree of life, we see
the flowing river and three precious materials: gold, bdellium,
which is pearl, and onyx, a precious stone. According to the further revelation of the Scriptures, especially Revelation 21, these
precious materials are for God's building.

Between Genesis and Revelation, the two ends of the Bible,
there is a wide gap, a broad span. What bridges this gap? The
bridge is the Gospel of John. The book of John opens with the
words, "In the beginning." However, if you read this gospel care-
fully, you will discover that the history recorded in it has no end.
Hence, it starts from the beginning in eternity past and it continues indefinitely into the future. Thus, it bridges the span

between Genesis and Revelation. (*Life-study of John,* pp. 1-2)

The divine building is the one Body, the one church, the one Bethel, the one corporate testimony of the Lord Himself. Eventually, there is the New Jerusalem as the completion. The New Jerusalem is not a physical place but a living composition of all of the living, redeemed ones in God, through the Spirit, having Christ as their life.

May the Lord reveal more and more to us concerning this building. I leave you with these two words: life and building. Life is for the building, and the building is of life. Life is the Lord Himself, and the building is the issue of the experience of the Lord as life. The more we experience the Lord as life, the more we realize the divine building among us. (*CWWL, 1963,* vol. 3, "The Building of God," p. 204)

When the Lord speaks of the Father's house in John 14, He is not referring to a heavenly mansion. The house in this chapter is the church. The church is God's house, the Father's house. The Lord Jesus spoke these words shortly before His death. Then through His death and resurrection, He built the church. This concept fits the entire thought of the Gospel of John.

The Gospel of John reveals that the Triune God is dispensing Himself into us, working Himself into us, by way of the Son's death and resurrection. The Lord Jesus indicated this in chapter 2 when He said to the Jewish leaders, "Destroy this temple, and in three days I will raise it up" (v. 19). The phrase *in three days* means in resurrection. Thus, here the Lord was saying that He would build up the temple, the Father's house, in resurrection. The Lord seemed to be telling the religious leaders, "You destroy this temple, My Father's house, and I will build it up in resurrection." (*The Fulfillment of the Tabernacle and the Offerings in the Writings of John,* pp. 337-338)

Further Reading: The Issue of Christ Being Glorified by the Father
with the Divine Glory, ch. 4; *The Fulfillment of the Tabernacle*
and the Offerings in the Writings of John, ch. 37

Enlightenment and inspiration: _____
_____
_____
_____

Morning Nourishment

John Jesus answered and said to them, Destroy this
2:19 temple, and in three days I will raise it up.
21-22 But He spoke of the temple of His body. When
       therefore He was raised from the dead, His disci-
       ples remembered that He had said this, and they
       believed the Scripture and the word which Jesus
       had spoken.

After Satan destroyed the Lord's physical body on the cross,
His body was put into a tomb and rested there. The Lord Jesus
then went into death, took a tour of the "Black House," and
came out in resurrection. When Jesus arose, He Himself raised
up His dead and buried body. The body of Jesus that was destroyed on the cross was small and weak; the Body of Christ in
resurrection is vast and powerful. Which do you prefer to
have—the body of Jesus or the Body of Christ? After the Lord's
resurrection, His Body, that is, the temple, was reared up on a
much larger scale. The body the enemy destroyed by crucifixion was merely the body of Jesus; what was raised by the Lord
in resurrection was not only His own body, but everyone who is
joined to Him by faith (1 Pet. 1:3; Eph. 2:6). After the Lord's resurrection, Satan would have had to say, "I lost my case. I was
stupid. I shouldn't have destroyed Him." Nevertheless, it was
too late for Satan to repent. (*Life-study of John*, pp. 85-86)

Today's Reading

When the Lord Jesus knew that the Jews were attempting to
destroy Him, He did not pray, "O Father, kill all these Jews. Father,
save Me and protect Me." Instead,…the Lord seemed to tell them,
"Do your best to kill Me. Be assured that after you put Me to death I
will have the opportunity to increase." No one can frustrate the
purpose of the Lord. The more the enemy tries to do, the more he
affords the opportunity for the Lord to do something more. Whatever the Lord does is always in resurrection. The Lord builds the
temple "in three days," signifying that He builds it in resurrection.

Since the day of His physical resurrection, the Lord Jesus has

been enlarging His Body in resurrection life. What an immense
Body Christ has today in His resurrection! Can you measure the
size of the Body of Christ? Although it once was possible to
measure the size of the physical body of Jesus, it is impossible to
measure the immensity of the Body of Christ. The Lord continues to build His Body in resurrection, and Satan keeps on help-
ing this. The house of God is still increasing in resurrection with
the Body of Christ (1 Tim. 3:15; 1 Pet. 2:5; 1 Cor. 3:9; Eph. 2:21-
22). Today, we are still within "the three days," because the Lord
is still working for the building of His Body under the process of
resurrection. A great part of the Lord's Body has already been
raised, but there are still some members of His Body who are not
yet raised. Therefore, the Lord's Body is still in the process of
resurrection. Even with yourself, only a part has been transformed, which means that only a part has been resurrected. The
Lord continues to work on you through the process of transformation. You are still in the process of resurrection. The church
today is still in the three days' process of resurrection.

In the changing of water into wine, the principle of life was
set forth. Now, in the dealing with the temple, the purpose of life
is shown. The principle of life is to change death into life. The
purpose of life is to build the house of God. The principle of life is
for the purpose of life....These two points govern the whole Gospel of John....Life is for the building. Life is for the church. It is
for the building of the church, His Body and God's house, that
the Lord has come to be our life. (*Life-study of John,* pp. 86-88)

Our living as Christians is simply a matter of the changing of
death into life for the building up of the mystical Body of Christ.
The entire Christian life consists of two matters: changing death
into life and building up the mystical Body of Christ. This is the
proper, genuine, and complete Christian life. (*The Fulfillment of
the Tabernacle and the Offerings in the Writings of John,* p. 54)

Further Reading: Life-study of John, msg. 7; *The Fulfillment of
the Tabernacle and the Offerings in the Writings of John,* ch. 5*

Enlightenment and inspiration: _____
_____
_____
_____

Morning Nourishment

John And the Word became flesh and tabernacled among
1:14 us (and we beheld His glory, glory as of the only
     Begotten from the Father), full of grace and reality.
14:23 Jesus answered and said..., If anyone loves Me, he
     will keep My word, and My Father will love him, and
     We will come to him and make an abode with him.

It is of vital importance that we see what the Father's house is. The Father's house is a matter of the Triune God—through incarnation, crucifixion, and resurrection—working Himself into His believers in order to be fully mingled with them that He may build them up as an organism for His dwelling place and expression. This is also for their dwelling place. Therefore, the sign of the Father's house points to the mingling of the Triune God with His redeemed people to produce a mutual dwelling place, a dwelling place for both God and His chosen and redeemed people. (*The Fulfillment of the Tabernacle and the Offerings in the Writings of John,* pp. 347-348)

Today's Reading

The first story in John 2 reveals the principle of the Lord's coming to be life to us; it is to bring life out of death, as signified by making wine out of water. Then the second story reveals the purpose of the Lord's coming to be life to us; it is for the building of the house of God. The way for the Lord to build up the house of God is to bring God into us and bring us into God to make us the abodes of God and to make God an abode for us, that is, to make God to dwell in us and us to dwell in Him so that God and we, we and God, become a mutual abode.

It is mostly John's books, his Gospel and his Epistles, that say that we are in God and He is in us, that is, that we abide in God and He abides in us. John 15:4, for example, says, "Abide in Me and I in you." This mutual abiding is accomplished by the work of Christ. Christ was incarnated to bring God into man, and He went back to God with man. When Christ came, He came with God to man. He came with a gift, a present, which is God

Himself. Then He went to God with a present for God, which is man. He came with God by incarnation, and He went with man by death and resurrection. His coming brought God into man, and His going brought man into God. By this coming and going He builds up the house of God by building God into man and man into God. By His coming and going He makes man the abode for God and makes God the abode for man. In this way, God and man, man and God, become a mutual abode. Then in the consummation of John's writings there is a building, the New Jerusalem, which is built up with God mingled with man.

By Christ, through Christ, and in Christ we are in God. This is the building of God mingled with humanity, which Christ accomplished by His death and resurrection. (*CWWL, 1963,* vol. 3, "The Building of God," pp. 199-201)

The Son of God, the Lord Jesus Christ, is not building a heavenly mansion. On the contrary, by the Spirit and through His death and resurrection, He is building an organism, the church, which is His Body and the Father's house. This house is composed of the mingling of the Triune God with His chosen and redeemed people.

The church in the New Testament is the second stage of the Father's house. The first stage of this house was God incarnate, God manifested in the flesh. The second stage is Christ resurrected with all His believers, the many sons built up together to be the church. Eventually, this church, the second stage of the Father's house, will consummate in the coming New Jerusalem. The New Jerusalem will be the ultimate consummation, the last stage, of the Father's house in the New Testament. Today we are neither in the first stage nor in the third but in the second. As those who are in the second stage, we are on our way to the third stage. (*The Fulfillment of the Tabernacle and the Offerings in the Writings of John,* pp. 344, 347)

Further Reading: The Fulfillment of the Tabernacle and the Offerings in the Writings of John, chs. 38-39; *CWWL, 1963,* vol. 3, "The Building of God," pp. 197-204

Enlightenment and inspiration: _____

_____

_____

_____

Hymns, #1221

1   Jesus, our wonderful Shepherd
     Brought us right out of the fold
  Into His pasture so plenteous,
     Into His riches untold.

    Glorious church life,
    Feasting from such a rich store!
    Here where we're dwelling in oneness
    God commands life evermore.

2   In the divisions He sought us,
     Weary and famished for food;
  Into the good land He brought us,
     Oh, to our spirit how good!

3   Jesus Himself is our pasture,
     He is the food that we eat;
  We as His sheep are fed richly
     Each time, whenever we meet.

4   Dwell we here on a high mountain,
     Wet with the morning-fresh dew,
  Slaking our thirst at the fountain,
     Water so living and new.

5   Christ is our rest and enjoyment,
     Here we have nothing to fear;
  Here all the sheep dwell securely,
     Kept by His presence so dear.

Composition for prophecy with main point and sub-points: _____

_____
_____
_____
_____
_____
_____
_____
_____
_____
_____
_____
_____
_____
_____
_____
_____
_____
_____
_____
_____
_____
_____
_____
_____
_____
_____
_____
_____
_____
_____
_____
_____
_____
_____
_____
_____
_____
_____
_____

The Vision of the Glorious Christ

Scripture Reading: Rev. 1:9—2:1, 7

Day 1

I. **The book of Revelation is "the revelation of Jesus Christ," and it is a book on the overcomers (1:1, 3; 2:7, 11, 17, 26-28; 3:5, 12, 20-21; 21:7; 22:18-19; 12:11):**
   A. The New Jerusalem is the totality of the overcomers:
      1. The overcomers will be the New Jerusalem in the coming age, the age of the millennial kingdom, as the precursor of the New Jerusalem in eternity (2:7; 3:12).
      2. In the New Jerusalem in eternity, all the believers will be overcomers (21:7).
   B. In the book of Revelation what the Lord wants and will build up is Zion, the overcomers (14:1; Psa. 51:18; 102:21; 128:5; 135:21; Isa. 41:27; Joel 3:17).

Day 2

   C. In order to be a constituent of Christ's overcoming bride (Rev. 19:7), we must see the vision of the glorious Christ in Revelation 1:
      1. We are on this earth for the word of God (the revealed Christ) and the testimony of Jesus (the testifying church) (vv. 2, 9-20; 19:10).
      2. We need to be in our spirit to receive the vision of the glorious Christ as the Son of Man in the midst of the golden lampstands (1:10, 13a; cf. 4:2; 17:3; 21:10).

Day 3

II. **Christ as the Son of Man is the High Priest, "clothed with a garment reaching to the feet, and girded about at the breasts with a golden girdle" (1:13), to cherish the churches in His humanity and nourish them in His divinity:**
   A. The Son of Man is Christ in His humanity, the golden girdle signifies His divinity, and breasts are a sign of love:
      1. Christ is girded at the loins, strengthened for the divine work (Exo. 28:4; Dan. 10:5) to produce the churches, but in Revelation 1 He

is girded about at the breasts, caring for the
churches that He has produced by His love.

2. The golden girdle signifies Christ's divinity
as His divine energy, and the breasts signify
that this golden energy is exercised and
motivated by and with His love to nourish
the churches.

B. Christ takes care of the churches in His humanity
as the Son of Man to cherish them (v. 13a):

1. He dresses the lamps of the lampstands to
make them proper, cherishing us so that we
may be happy, pleasant, and comfortable
(Exo. 30:7; cf. Psa. 42:5, 11):

a. The Lord's presence provides an atmosphere of tenderness and warmth to cherish our being, giving us rest, comfort,
healing, cleansing, and encouragement.

b. We can enjoy the cherishing atmosphere
of the Lord's presence in the church to
receive the nourishing supply of life (Eph.
5:29; cf. 1 Tim. 4:6; Eph. 4:11).

2. He trims the wicks of the lamps of the lampstand, cutting off all the negative things that
frustrate our shining (Exo. 25:38):

a. The charred part of the wick, the snuff,
signifies things that are not according to
God's purpose and need to be cut off, such
as our flesh, our natural man, our self,
and our old creation.

b. He trims away all the differences among
the churches (the wrongdoings, short-
ages, failures, and defects) so that they
may be the same in essence, appearance,
and expression (cf. 1 Cor. 1:10; 2 Cor.
12:18; Phil. 2:2).

Day 4   C. Christ takes care of the churches in His divinity
with His divine love, signified by the golden
girdle at His breasts, to nourish the churches
(Rev. 1:13b):

  1. He nourishes us with Himself as the all-inclusive Christ in His full ministry of three stages so that we may grow and mature in the divine life to be His overcomers to accomplish His eternal economy.
  2. As the walking Christ, He gets to know the condition of each church, and as the speaking Spirit, He trims and fills the lampstands with fresh oil, the supply of the Spirit (2:1, 7).
  3. To participate in His move and enjoy His care we must be in the churches.

III. **The heavenly ancientness of the Lord is depicted by His head and hair being white as white wool, as snow (1:14; Dan. 7:9; Job 15:10; cf. S. S. 5:11).**

IV. **The Lord's seven eyes are like a flame of fire for watching, observing, searching, judging by enlightening, and infusing (Rev. 1:14; 5:6; Dan. 10:6):**

  A. Christ's eyes are for God's move and operation on earth, since seven is the number for completion in God's move.
  B. The Lord's eyes being like a flame of fire is mainly for His judgment (7:9-10; Rev. 2:18; 19:11-12).

Day 5 V. **The Lord's feet are like shining bronze, as having been fired in a furnace, signifying that His perfect and bright walk qualifies Him to exercise divine judgment (1:15; Ezek. 1:7; Dan. 10:6).**

VI. **The Lord's voice is like the sound of many waters (Rev. 1:15; cf. 14:2), which is a tumultuous sound, the sound of the voice of the Almighty God (Ezek. 1:24; 43:2) in its seriousness and solemnity (cf. Rev. 10:3).**

VII. **Christ is the Holder of the bright messengers of the churches (1:16a, 20):**

  A. The messengers are the spiritual ones in the churches, the ones who bear the responsibility of the testimony of Jesus.

B. The messengers, who are of the heavenly nature and in a heavenly position like stars, are those who have a fresh message from the Lord to His people (2:1a).

C. Because the leading ones are in His right hand, there is no need for them to shrink back; Christ truly takes the responsibility for His testimony.

Day 6 VIII. **Out of Christ's mouth proceeds a sharp two-edged sword, which is His discerning, judging, and slaying word for dealing with negative persons and things (1:16b; Heb. 4:12; Eph. 6:17).**

IX. **Christ's face is as the sun shining in its power (Dan. 10:6) for judging enlightenment to bring in the kingdom (Rev. 1:16c; Matt. 17:2; cf. Mal. 4:2; Judg. 5:31; Matt. 13:43).**

X. **Christ is the First and the Last, assuring us that He will never leave His work unfinished, and the living One for the churches as the expression of His Body to be living, fresh, and strong (Rev. 1:17-18a).**

XI. **Christ has the keys of death and of Hades (v. 18b):**

A. Death is a collector and Hades is a keeper, but Christ nullified death on the cross and overcame Hades in His resurrection (2 Tim. 1:10; Acts 2:24).

B. As long as we give the Lord the ground, the opportunity, and the way to move and act among us by exercising to deny the self, take up the cross, and lose our soul-life, death and Hades will be under His control (Matt. 16:18, 21-26).

Morning Nourishment

Rev. The revelation of Jesus Christ which God gave to
1:1 Him to show to His slaves the things that must
quickly take place; and He made *it* known by signs,
sending *it* by His angel to His slave John.
2:7 He who has an ear, let him hear what the Spirit
says to the churches. To him who overcomes, to
him I will give to eat of the tree of life, which is in
the Paradise of God.

"The revelation of Jesus Christ" [in Revelation 1:1] means
that this revelation is of Jesus Christ, through Jesus Christ, and
concerning Jesus Christ. God first gave this revelation to Jesus
Christ and then gave this revelation to us through Him. All the
revelations in the Bible are focused on Jesus Christ and are for
the purpose of revealing Him. Hence, the book of Revelation not
only shows us future events, but who the person of Jesus Christ
is....It shows us this One, who was once Jesus of Nazareth in the
world and who is now the Christ exalted to the heavens....The
goal of Revelation is that more people would know such a Christ
so that they would be watchful until the day when they can see
Him face to face. (*CWWN,* vol. 34, p. 163)

Today's Reading

The entire Scripture composed of sixty-six books concludes
with two things: the overcomers and the New Jerusalem. These
are the two main items revealed in the book of Revelation, the last
book of the Bible. Revelation 1—20 gives us a complete record of
the overcomers, and the New Jerusalem in Revelation 21—22
will be the issue, the coming out, the consummation, of the overcomers. The New Jerusalem will be manifested in two stages. The
first stage will be in the millennium, the one-thousand-year kingdom. That will be the precursor of the New Jerusalem in the new
heaven and new earth for eternity, the second stage of the New
Jerusalem in the eternal age.

The New Jerusalem is the totality of the overcomers. The
overcomers will be the New Jerusalem in the coming age, the

age of the millennium....Only a relatively small part of the believers will be the overcomers. The majority of the believers—
genuine, regenerated, blood-washed believers—will have been
defeated. At the Lord's coming, He will take away only the overcomers, leaving the rest of the believers in another category
because they will not have the maturity in His divine life. In the
millennium the overcoming believers will be with Christ in the
bright glory of the kingdom, whereas the defeated believers will
suffer discipline in outer darkness (Matt. 8:12; 22:13; 25:30).
This is so that they can be perfected for their maturity.

For any crop to become matured, that crop needs to go through
a certain process. The process through which the immature believers will have to pass will not be pleasant but will be a period of discipline and punishment for one thousand years....[This process]
will complete God's eternal economy. All of these dear ones will be
matured and perfected. After the thousand years, the Lord will
clear up the entire universe through His judgment at the great
white throne (Rev. 20:11-15). Then there will be the new heaven
and the new earth with the New Jerusalem. The New Jerusalem
in eternity will be greatly enlarged to include all the believers. By
then all the believers will be overcomers (Rev. 21:7).

The earlier overcomers will be rewarded. The Lord will
reward the overcomers in this age with what they are in Christ.
They will enjoy their victory, but the defeated ones who were not
ready will have nothing to enjoy as their reward. Instead, the
Lord will deal with them so that they can become matured and
perfected. Eventually, the majority of the believers will enjoy
what they are in Christ for eternity.

We can prove this according to our experience. When we are
victorious in the Lord, we enjoy our victory every day, but when
we are defeated, the enjoyment of the Lord is gone....What we
would, could, and should enjoy in the Lord will be what we are.
(*The Overcomers,* pp. 9-11)

Further Reading: The Overcomers, ch. 1; *CWWN,* vol. 11, pp. 760-763

Enlightenment and inspiration: _____

_____

_____
_____

Morning Nourishment

Rev. Who testified the word of God and the testimony of
1:2   Jesus Christ, *even* all that he saw.
   9 I John, your brother and fellow partaker in the
      tribulation and kingdom and endurance in Jesus,
      was on the island called Patmos because of the
      word of God and the testimony of Jesus.

John was known as the disciple who reclined on the Lord's breast (John 13:25; 21:20). Yet the King on the throne was unfamiliar to John. God revealed such a Jesus Christ to John. This knowledge is fundamental. Once John had this knowledge, the prophecies and the future events were not hard to deal with.

Under what conditions did John see this vision? Revelation 1:9 says, "I John, your brother and fellow partaker in the tribulation and kingdom and endurance in Jesus, was on the island called Patmos because of the word of God and the testimony of Jesus." John received his revelation under this circumstance. He did not say that he was a great apostle chosen by the Lord....He did not consider himself higher than others. He considered himself as our brother. How humble and gentle this is. Although his body was on the island of Patmos, his spirit was suffering, enduring, and waiting for the coming of the kingdom together with his brothers. He felt this way because he lived in the reality of the Body. (*CWWN,* vol. 34, pp. 163-164)

Today's Reading

[John] knew that the tribulation, kingdom, and endurance are three inseparable things. Before the kingdom comes, there will surely be tribulations. Through many tribulations we will enter the kingdom of God (Acts 14:22). Tribulations paved the way for John to enter the kingdom, and these tribulations worked out for him, more and more surpassingly, an eternal weight of glory (2 Cor. 4:17). He aspired for the kingdom, and therefore, he did not shrink from the tribulations. The kingdom will come, but it is still not here. If we do not endure, we will slumber, withdraw, or turn to the enticements of the world. John knew this; therefore, he waited patiently. He believed that his brothers would become fellow partakers in the tribulation and kingdom and endurance in Jesus. Praise the Lord! He was not alone in his way.

Are we fellow partakers in the tribulation and kingdom and endurance in Jesus?...Do we identify ourselves with John's feelings and experience, or are we those who have chosen the broad pathway and who are traveling on our own?...We do not enter the kingdom simply by believing that there is a kingdom. We cannot enter the kingdom simply by having some knowledge about the kingdom. In order to enter the kingdom, we have to take John's way. Otherwise, our entry into the kingdom will only be a theory.

John was exiled to the island of Patmos because he was faithful to God's word and because he was for the testimony of Jesus. This island was in the middle of the ocean, with precipitous rocks and barrenness on all sides. John was put in an uninhabited spot. Humanly speaking, this was lonely and pitiful! However, John did not murmur at all. He knew whom he was suffering for. Thank and praise God. Under such circumstances, the glorious Christ revealed Himself to him and gave him new revelations. The earth had diminished before John's eyes, but heaven was opened to him! This brings to mind Joseph who was in prison, Moses who was in the wilderness, David who was in distress, and Paul who was in chains. They all received fresh revelations. John was going down the path they had trodden; he received visions that he had never received before, and he came to know the enthroned Lord whom he had never known before. (*CWWN*, vol. 34, pp. 164-165)

On one hand, this book gives us the revelation of Christ, and on the other hand, it shows us the testimony of Jesus, which is the church. It presents to us the revealed Christ and the testifying church....This testimony of Jesus is the spirit—the substance, the disposition, and the characteristic—of the prophecy (Rev. 19:10). (Rev. 1:2, footnote 1)

Further Reading: CWWN, vol. 34, pp. 163-187

Enlightenment and inspiration: _____

_____

_____

_____

Morning Nourishment

Rev. **And in the midst of the lampstands One like the**
1:13 **Son of Man, clothed with a garment reaching to**
      the feet, and girded about at the breasts with a
      golden girdle.
Exo. **...Every morning when he dresses the lamps...**
30:7
Eph. **For no one ever hated his own flesh, but nourishes**
5:29 **and cherishes it, even as Christ also the church.**

To cherish people is to make them happy and to make them feel pleasant and comfortable. We must have a pleasant countenance when we contact people. We should be happy and rejoicing....We must give people the impression that we are genuinely happy and pleasant. Otherwise, we will not be able to cherish them, to make them happy.

Then we should go on to nourish them. We do not nourish people when we speak to them about marriage, courtship, politics, the world situation, or education. To nourish people is to feed them with the all-inclusive Christ in His full ministry in three stages.

In order to nourish people with Christ, we first have to seek Christ, experience Christ, gain Christ, enjoy Christ, and participate in Christ. (*The Vital Groups,* pp. 102-103)

Today's Reading

Christ is the best model of cherishing and nourishing as seen in Revelation 1....[Verses 12 and 13 show] that Christ is taking care of the lampstands by being the Son of Man with a long garment. This garment is the priestly robe (Exo. 28:33-35), which shows that Christ is our great High Priest.

He is also girded about at the breasts with a golden girdle. This girdle is a long piece of gold. The girdle and the gold are not two separate things. The girdle is the gold. The golden girdle is one piece of gold to become a belt. The Son of Man is in His humanity, and the golden girdle signifies His divinity. This golden girdle is on His breasts, and the breasts are a sign of love.

The priests in the Old Testament were girded at the loins for their ministry (Exo. 28:4). In Daniel 10:5 Christ also is girded at His loins, with fine gold. To be girded at the loins is to be strengthened for the work. Christ has finished His divine work in producing the churches. Now by His love He is caring for the churches which He has produced. This is why He is girded at the breasts. Today Christ is our High Priest taking care of His churches established by His labor....I hope we all could realize that in these days, even among us, Christ is wearing a golden girdle on His breasts.

A piece of gold is now a girdle. The totality of Christ in His divinity has become a girdle. The golden girdle signifies Christ's divinity becoming His energy, and the breasts signify that this golden energy is exercised and motivated by His love. His divine energy is exercised by and with His love to nourish the churches.

Christ takes care of the churches as the lampstands in His humanity as "the Son of Man" to cherish them (Rev. 1:13a). Christ as our High Priest takes care of the churches He has established first in His humanity to cherish the churches, to make the churches happy, pleasant, and comfortable.

He does this by dressing the lamps of the lampstand. The high priest in the Old Testament dressed the lamps of the lampstands every morning (Exo. 30:7). To dress the lamps is to make them proper.

Christ cares for the lampstands by trimming the wicks of the lamps of the lampstand, just as the priest did according to the type in the Old Testament (Exo. 25:38). When the wick was burned out, it became charred and black, so the priest had to come to cut off the black part of the wick....The charred part of the wick, the snuff, signifies things that are not according to God's purpose which need to be cut off, such as our flesh, our natural man, our self, and our old creation. All the lampstands are organic. They are living lampstands. Since each church is a living lampstand, each church has much feeling. A church with charred wicks will not feel comfortable. (*The Vital Groups,* pp. 105-106)

Further Reading: The Vital Groups, msgs. 7, 10-11

Enlightenment and inspiration: _____

_____

_____

_____

Morning Nourishment

Rev.   And in the midst of the lampstands One like the Son
1:13-14   of Man,...girded about at the breasts with a golden
girdle. And His head and hair were as white as white
wool, as snow; and His eyes were like a flame of fire.
Dan.   I watched until thrones were set, and the Ancient
7:9   of Days sat down. His clothing was like white snow,
and the hair of His head was like pure wool; His
throne was flames of fire, its wheels, burning fire.

Christ, as the High Priest, takes care of the churches as the
lampstands in His divinity with His divine love, signified by the
golden girdle on His breasts, to nourish the churches (Rev.
1:13b). Christ is not only human but also divine. He is the Son of
Man wearing a golden girdle, signifying His divinity as His
divine energy. His divinity as the divine energy nourishes the
churches in many ways....He is also the High Priest with His
divinity as the "energy belt" to nourish us with Himself as the
all-inclusive Christ in His full ministry of three stages....In His
divinity He is nourishing us so that we may grow and mature in
the divine life to be His overcomers to accomplish His eternal
economy. (*The Vital Groups,* pp. 107, 109)

Today's Reading

White hair signifies great age (Job 15:10). The black hair with
which the Lord is depicted in Song of Songs 5:11 signifies His
unfading and everlasting strength, but the white hair with which
He is depicted [in Revelation 1:14] signifies His ancientness.

Although Christ is ancient, He is not old. In this chapter we
see that His head and His hair were white as wool and as snow.
White wool issues from the nature of life, and white snow comes
down from the sky, from heaven. Wool is not made white; it is born
white, and its whiteness comes out of its nature. White wool is the
color of Christ's nature....Snow is white because it comes from
heaven and contains no earthly dirt or stain. Hence, white wool,
both here and in Daniel 7:9, signifies that the ancientness of
Christ is of His nature, not of His becoming old, while white snow

signifies that His ancientness is heavenly, not earthly.

In Revelation 1:14, we see that His eyes are as a flame of fire.... This is for Him to observe and search in His judging by enlightening. In this book His eyes are not two but seven (5:6). Seven is the number of completion in God's move. Hence, His eyes in this book are for God's operation. These seven eyes of His are the "seven lamps of fire burning before the throne, which are the seven Spirits of God" (4:5; cf. Dan. 10:6). The "fire burning" equals the "flame of fire" and is for observing and searching. The seven Spirits of God which are sent forth into all the earth are also for God's move upon the earth. Thus, the eyes of Christ in this book are the seven Spirits of God for God's move and operation on earth today.

Christ's eyes are for watching, observing, searching, judging by enlightening, and infusing. We must experience all these different aspects of His eyes, especially the aspect of infusing. His eyes infuse us with all that He is. His infusing eyes are a flame of fire which is continually burning....Since the day we were saved, Christ's eyes have been like a burning fire enlightening and infusing us. His eyes also stir us up to be hot. After Christ has looked at us, we can never be cold as we once were. By looking at us, He burns us and stirs us up in the Lord. Many times the Lord comes to us with His piercing eyes....When I was arguing with others, especially with my intimate ones, the shining eyes of Christ were upon me, and I could not go on speaking. His shining stopped my mouth.

The book of Revelation is a book with a judging nature. Fire is for divine judgment (1 Cor. 3:13; Heb. 6:8; 10:27). "Our God is also a consuming fire" (Heb. 12:29). His throne is like the fiery flame and its wheels as burning fire, and a fiery stream issues and comes forth from before Him (Dan. 7:9-10). All this is for judgment. The main significance of the Lord's eyes being as a flame of fire is for His judgment (Rev. 2:18-23; 19:11-12). When He comes to take possession of the earth by exercising judgment over it, even His feet will be like pillars of fire (10:1). (*Life-study of Revelation*, pp. 104-106)

Further Reading: The Mending Ministry of John, ch. 14

Enlightenment and inspiration: _____

_____

_____

_____

Morning Nourishment

Rev. **And His feet were like shining bronze, as having**
1:15-16 **been fired in a furnace; and His voice was like the**
sound of many waters. And He had in His right
hand seven stars...
Dan. **...His arms and His feet like the gleam of polished**
10:6 **bronze, and the sound of His words like the sound**
of a multitude.

Revelation 1:15 says, "His feet were like shining bronze, as having been fired in a furnace." Feet signify the walk. In typology, bronze signifies divine judgment (Exo. 27:1-6). When Christ was on earth, His earthly walk and daily walk were tried and tested. Because His walk was tested, He came out shining. Now the feet of Christ are as shining bronze, as mentioned also in Ezekiel 1:7 and Daniel 10:6, signifying that His perfect and bright walk qualifies Him to exercise divine judgment. To be "fired in a furnace" is to be tried by being burned. Christ's walk was tried by His sufferings, even by His death on the cross. Hence, His walk is bright as the shining bronze, which qualifies Him to judge the unrighteous....When He comes to possess the earth by judging it, His feet will be like pillars of fire (Rev. 10:1). (*Life-study of Revelation,* p. 106)

Today's Reading

Revelation 1:15 also says that "His voice" is "like the sound of many waters." "The sound of many waters," a tumultuous sound, is the sound of the voice of the Almighty God (Ezek. 1:24; 43:2). It signifies the seriousness and solemnity of His speaking (cf. Rev. 10:3). Sometimes the Lord's voice is gentle and tender, but at other times His voice shocks us like thunder. Whenever we are sloppy or sleepy, the voice of the Lord will wake us up. His voice, which is that of the Almighty God, warns us and wakes us up.

Revelation 1:16 says, "He had in His right hand seven stars." As verse 20 makes clear, "the seven stars are the messengers of the seven churches." The messengers are the spiritual ones in the churches bearing the responsibility of the testimony of Jesus.

Like stars, they should be of the heavenly nature and in a heavenly position. In the Acts and the Epistles the elders were the leading ones in the operation of the local churches (Acts 14:23; 20:17; Titus 1:5). The eldership is somewhat official, and, as we have seen, at the time this book was written the offices in the churches had deteriorated in the degradation of the church. In this book the Lord calls our attention back to spiritual reality. Hence, it emphasizes the messengers of the churches rather than the elders. The office of the elders is easily perceived, but the believers need to see the importance of the spiritual and heavenly reality of the messengers for the proper church life to bear the testimony of Jesus in the darkness of the church's degradation.

Both the lampstands and the stars are for shining in the night. A lampstand representing a local church is a collective unit, whereas a star representing a messenger of a local church is an individual entity. In the dark night of the church's degradation, there is the need of the shining both of the collective churches and of the individual messengers. As Christ walks among the churches, He holds the leading ones in His right hand. How comforting this is! The leading ones must praise Him that they are in His hands and that He is holding them. Since the leading ones are in His hands, there is no need for them to shrink back, to be weak, or to be mistaken. Christ truly takes the responsibility for His testimony.

In the book of Revelation there are no elders in the churches; rather, there are messengers. At the time this book was written, the church had become degraded. Hence, in Revelation, the Lord repudiates all formalities. Being an elder may be somewhat legal or formal. Do not aspire to be an elder; desire to be a shining star. Do not be one with a mere position—be a shining star. Both the lampstand and the stars shine at night. Both the church and the leading ones in the churches must shine. All the leading ones must be stars. (*Life-study of Revelation,* pp. 106-108)

Further Reading: Life-study of Revelation, msg. 9

Enlightenment and inspiration: _____

_____

_____

_____

Morning Nourishment

Rev. **...Out of His mouth proceeded a sharp two-edged**
1:16-18 **sword; and His face *shone* as the sun shines in its**
power. And when I saw Him, I fell at His feet as
dead; and He placed His right hand on me, saying,
Do not fear; I am the First and the Last and the liv-
ing One; and I became dead, and behold, I am
living forever and ever; and I have the keys of
death and of Hades.

In Revelation 1:16 we are told that "out of His mouth proceeded a sharp two-edged sword." In Song of Songs 5:16, "His
mouth is sweetness itself," and in the Gospels, "words of grace"
proceeded out of His mouth (Luke 4:22); but here "out of His
mouth proceeded a sharp two-edged sword." This is His discerning, judging, "and slaying word" (Heb. 4:12; Eph. 6:17). The
"words of grace" are for His supply of grace to His favored ones,
whereas the "sharp two-edged sword" is for His dealing with
negative persons and things....Because of the church's degradation, we all need a certain amount of judgment....The words
which proceed out of the Lord's mouth are sharp, piercing into
our being, dividing our soul from our spirit, and discerning the
intents of our heart. (*Life-study of Revelation,* p. 108)

Today's Reading

In Revelation 1:16 we are also told that "His face shone as the
sun shines in its power,"...as in Daniel 10:6, for the judging
enlightenment to bring in the kingdom. When He was transfigured and His face shone as the sun, that was His coming in the
kingdom (Matt. 16:28—17:2). When He comes to take over the
earth for the kingdom, His face will be as the sun (Rev. 10:1).

Revelation 1:17 says, "And when I saw Him, I fell at His feet
as dead; and He placed His right hand on me, saying, Do not
fear; I am the First and the Last." Christ is not only the First and
the Last, but also the beginning and the ending. This assures us
that, having started the church life, He will surely accomplish it.
He will never leave His work unfinished. All the local churches

must believe that the Lord Jesus is the beginning and the ending. He will accomplish what He has begun in His recovery.

In verse 18 we see that the Lord is "the living One," the One who "became dead" and who is "living forever and ever." The very Christ who walks in the midst of the churches, who is the Head of the churches and to whom the churches belong, is the living One full of life. Hence, the churches as His Body should also be living and full of life. Hallelujah, we have a living Christ who has overcome death! Our Christ, who is the resurrected Christ, is living in us and among us. He is living forever and ever. What a living Christ we have in the recovery! In the recovery, all the churches should be as living as Christ, full of life and overcoming death.

In verse 18 the Lord also said, "I have the keys of death and of Hades." Due to the fall and sin of man, death came in and is now working on earth to gather up all the sinful people. Death resembles a dustpan used to collect the dust from the floor, and Hades resembles a trash can. Whatever the dustpan collects is put into the trash can. Thus, death is a collector and Hades is a keeper. In the church life today are we still subject to death and Hades? No! Christ abolished death on the cross and overcame Hades in His resurrection. Although Hades tried its best to hold Him, it was powerless to do it (Acts 2:24). With Him, death has no sting and Hades has no power....In the church life, the keys of death and Hades are in His hand. It is impossible for us to deal with death; we simply do not have the ability to handle it. Whenever death enters, it will deaden many. But as long as we give the Lord Jesus the ground, the opportunity, and the free way to move and act among us, both death and Hades will be under His control. However, whenever the Lord Jesus does not have the ground in the church, death immediately becomes prevailing and Hades becomes powerful to hold the dead ones. Praise the Lord that Christ has the keys of death and Hades. Death is subject to Him and Hades is under His control. Hallelujah! (*Life-study of Revelation*, pp. 110-111)

Further Reading: Life-study of Revelation, msg. 9

Enlightenment and inspiration: _____

_____

_____

_____

Hymns, #1184

1   In Revelation chapter one
God gives a vision of the Son,
Of Him who was and is to come;
Oh, let us to this One now come.

2   In spirit hear His trumpet voice;
We must be turned to see His choice—
The seven lampstands golden fair;
The Son of Man is walking there.

3   The great high priestly robe He wears,
For every church He fully cares:
He trims the lamp, the oil supplies;
He makes them burn, flames in His eyes.

4   A golden girdle on His breast—
His work is done, and from His rest
He unto all the churches pours
Himself in love, the treasure store.

5   His head, His hair is white as wool—
The ancient One with youth is full.
His face is shining as the sun
To burn and lighten every one.

6   Oh, when this living One we see,
We'll fall as dead, we'll finished be.
But then the Lord His comfort gives—
He once was dead, but now He lives.

7   Let every church just love Him more—
His riches then He will outpour.
All other loves now lay aside;
Let's take this Jesus, none beside.

Composition for prophecy with main point and sub-points: _____

_____
_____
_____
_____
_____
_____
_____
_____
_____
_____
_____
_____
_____
_____
_____
_____
_____
_____
_____
_____
_____
_____
_____
_____
_____
_____
_____
_____
_____
_____
_____
_____
_____
_____
_____
_____

Christ's Heavenly Priesthood
Ministered to the Churches
for the Producing of the Overcomers

Scripture Reading: Rev. 2—3

Day 1
I. **Christ's heavenly priesthood is a speaking ministry:**

   A. Christ speaks to God to intercede for us, and He speaks to us to minister the priestly service (Heb. 7:25; Rev. 1:16, 20; 2:1a, 7; cf. Mal. 3:1; Heb. 1:2):

   1. No one has ever seen God; the Son, as the Word of God (John 1:1, 14) and the speaking of God, has declared Him with a full expression, explanation, and definition of Him (v. 18).

   2. The book of Revelation tells us that even in the warfare for the kingdom of God, Christ is the Word of God speaking for God's purpose (19:13).

   B. By Christ's walking in the midst of the churches, He gets to know the condition of each church; such a tour of the churches makes Him thoroughly familiar with every situation; then according to what He sees, He speaks to us (2:1, 7).

   C. In His walking He is Christ, and in His speaking He is the Spirit; at the beginning of each of the seven epistles it is the Lord who speaks (vv. 1, 8, 12, 18; 3:1, 7, 14), and at the end it is the Spirit speaking to the churches (2:7, 11, 17, 29; 3:6, 13, 22); the walking Christ becomes the speaking Spirit.

Day 2
   D. The nature of the Lord's priestly speaking is to trim and fill the golden lampstands:

   1. In the Old Testament there was the lampstand in the tabernacle; every morning the lamps were trimmed by having their charred wicks snuffed (Exo. 30:7); in addition, the lamps were supplied with oil (27:20).

   2. To trim is to cut off the charred ends that can no longer burn brightly; to add oil is to supply the Spirit.

     3. In Revelation 2 and 3 our High Priest is trimming the seven lampstands, cutting away those things that are not needed and that frustrate the shining; at the same time He is supplying the oil that is needed and that will make the lampstands burn brightly.

II. **The Lord's speaking trims away religion (2:9):**
  A. Today's Christianity has been Judaized; there are many essential differences between Judaism and the church in four major points—the temple, the law, the priests, and the worldly promises:
    1. In Judaism there is a material temple, whereas the temple in the church is a spiritual temple; in Judaism the worshippers and the place of worship are two different things; there is no place of worship in the church, for the place of worship is the worshipper (Eph. 2:21-22; John 4:24; 1 Cor. 3:16; 6:19; 2 Cor. 6:16).
    2. In Judaism there are the laws, a standard of principles for daily living, which are written on tablets of stone; in the church the Holy Spirit is our indwelling law of life inscribed on our hearts (Heb. 8:10).
    3. In Judaism there is a mediatorial class of priests, but in the church all the believers are laboring priests of the gospel of God, a holy and royal priesthood (Rom. 15:16; Rev. 1:6; 1 Pet. 2:5, 9).
    4. In Judaism there are worldly promises and earthly blessings, but in the church there are heavenly promises and spiritual blessings (Eph. 1:3; Gal. 3:14; cf. Matt. 16:24).
  B. "He is a not Jew who is one outwardly; neither is circumcision that which is outward in the flesh. But he is a Jew who is one inwardly; and circumcision is of the heart, in spirit, not in letter, whose praise is not from men, but from God" (Rom. 2:28-29; cf. Phil. 3:3; Gal. 3:7, 14, 16, 29).

Day 3 III. **The Lord's speaking trims away worldliness (Rev. 2:12-17):**

A. Satan's throne is in the world, the place where he dwells and the sphere of his reign; since the worldly church entered into union with the world, she dwells where Satan's throne is (v. 13; cf. John 12:31-33; 14:30).

B. The worldly and degraded church holds not only the teaching of Balaam but also the teaching of the Nicolaitans; the teaching of Balaam distracts people from the person of Christ to idolatry and from the enjoyment of Christ to spiritual fornication, whereas the teaching of the Nicolaitans destroys the function of the believers as members of the Body of Christ, thus annulling the Lord's Body as His expression; the former teaching disregards the Head, and the latter destroys the Body (Rev. 2:14-15).

C. While the church goes the way of the world, the overcomers come forward to abide in the presence of God in the Holy of Holies, where they enjoy the hidden Christ as a special portion for their daily supply; if we seek the Lord, overcome the degradation of the worldly church, and enjoy a special portion of the Lord today, He as the hidden manna will be a reward to us in the coming kingdom (vv. 16-17).

Day 4 IV. **The Lord's speaking trims away the leaven of the evil in the apostate church (vv. 18-29):**

A. The woman Jezebel is the same as the one prophesied by the Lord in Matthew 13:33; there the woman added leaven (signifying evil, heretical, and pagan things) into the fine flour (signifying Christ as the meal offering for the satisfaction of God and man).

B. This woman is the great harlot of Revelation 17, who mixes abominations with the divine things; Jezebel, the pagan wife of Ahab, is a type of the apostate church (2:20; 1 King 16:31; 19:1-2; 21:23, 25-26; 2 Kings 9:7).

C. We need to beware of the principle of Babylon, the principle of the apostate church; anything that is halfway and not absolute is called Babylon; we need God to enlighten us so that in His light we may judge everything in us that is not absolute toward Him (Rev. 3:16-19; cf. Num. 6:1-9):

   1. The principle of Babylon (Heb. *Babel*) is man's endeavor to build up something from earth to heaven by human ability, signified by bricks (Gen. 11:1-9; 1 Cor. 3:12).

   Day 5   2. The principle of Babylon is hypocrisy (Rev. 17:4, 6; Matt. 23:25-32; 6:1-6; 15:7-8; John 5:44; 12:42-43).

   3. The principle of Babylon is that of not considering herself a widow but of glorifying herself and living luxuriously; in a sense, the believers in Christ are a widow in the present age because their Husband, Christ, is absent from them; because our Beloved is not here in the world, our heart is not here (Rev. 18:7; cf. 1 Cor. 16:22; Rev. 22:20; Luke 12:34; 1 Tim. 6:6-10).

   4. The principle of Babylon is the principle of a harlot; Babylon's purpose is for man to make a name for himself and deny God's name; the church, as the pure virgin espoused to Christ, should have no name other than her Husband's (Gen. 11:4; Rev. 3:8; 2 Cor. 11:2; 1 Cor. 1:10).

V. **The Lord's speaking trims away lukewarmness (Rev. 3:14-22):**

A. "I know your works, that you are neither cold nor hot; I wish that you were cold or hot. So, because you are lukewarm and neither hot nor cold, I am about to spew you out of My mouth" (vv. 15-16).

B. Laodicea is a distorted Philadelphia (vv. 14-22):

   1. When brotherly love is gone, Philadelphia immediately turns into "the opinion of the people" (the meaning of *Laodicea*).

    2. Laodicea is characterized by lukewarmness and spiritual pride; spiritual pride comes from history; some were once rich, and they think that they are still rich; the Lord was once merciful to them, and they remember their history, but now they have lost that reality.

Day 6
    3. Laodicea means to know everything but in reality to be fervent about nothing; in name it has everything, but it cannot sacrifice its life for anything; it remembers its former glory but forgets its present condition before God.

    4. If we want to continue in the way of Philadelphia and be saved from the lukewarmness of Laodicea, we must remember to humble ourselves before God (Isa. 66:1-2; 57:15).

VI. **In addition to trimming the lampstand, the priest also filled the lamps with oil; to eat of the tree of life, to eat of the hidden manna, and to feast with the Lord are all the infilling of the Spirit (cf. Zech. 4:11-14):**

    A. The book of Revelation reveals the intensification of the Triune God (1:4; 3:1; 4:5; 5:6) to bring the degraded church back to the enjoyment of Himself as the tree of life, the hidden manna, and the feast for the finalization of God's New Testament economy.

    B. "To him who overcomes, to him I will give to eat of the tree of life, which is in the Paradise of God" (2:7); eating of the tree of life is the best infilling.

    C. "To him who overcomes, to him I will give of the hidden manna" (v. 17); to eat of the hidden manna is to be filled and supplied.

    D. "Behold, I stand at the door and knock; if anyone hears My voice and opens the door, then I will come in to him and dine with him and he with Me" (3:20); by feasting with the Lord, the infilling takes place.

VII. By Christ's high priestly service all the dark
things of religion, worldliness, evil, and lukewarmness are trimmed away; also by His heavenly priesthood the heavenly, divine element
of the tree of life, the hidden manna, and the
heavenly feast is ministered to us; the effect
of this heavenly ministry is a metabolic transformation to make us precious stones for the
building of God's dwelling place (Rom. 12:2;
2 Cor. 3:18):

A. All the Lord's heavenly service and care have the
aim of making us the overcomers (Rev. 2:7, 11, 17,
26-28; 3:5, 12, 20-21).

B. The nourishment of the tree of life, the hidden
manna, and the heavenly feast becomes the divine
element of which the lampstand is composed.

C. Thus, every local church will be a lampstand, and
in every local church there will be overcomers;
these overcomers will make up the lampstand; a
lampstand eventually is the overcomers in a local
church.

VIII. While the Lord Jesus is arranging the world
situation so that God's people may go on, He
is also exercising His heavenly ministry to
especially supply God's lovers and seekers
with the heavenly riches, the divine element,
so that they may be kept at an overcoming
level; the sustaining of these God-lovers and
Christ-seekers needs Christ's heavenly ministry (Acts 5:31; Heb. 7:25; 8:2).

Morning Nourishment

Heb. Hence also He is able to save to the uttermost those
7:25 who come forward to God through Him, since He
      lives always to intercede for them.
Rev. ...And out of His mouth proceeded a sharp two-
1:16 edged sword...
 2:1 ...These things says He who holds the seven stars
      in His right hand, He who walks in the midst of the
      seven golden lampstands.

[Revelation 1] clearly depicts Christ as our High Priest, wearing
the priestly robe which signifies that He is ministering of Himself
and of the divine nature and life into us....You may think that in
chapters 2 and 3 the Lord is dealing with the seven churches, and
not associate this with His priestly service....[However], chapters
2 and 3 show how He ministers the priestly service to us.

This ministry of the priestly service is accomplished mainly
by His speaking. Christ's heavenly priesthood is a speaking ministry. In my early Christian life I thought that Christ was in the
heavens only interceding for us as our High Priest....He speaks
to God to intercede for us, and He [also] speaks to us to minister
the priestly service. (*The Mending Ministry of John,* p. 119)

Today's Reading

John, in his last writing, Revelation, tells us that even in the
warfare for the kingdom of God, Christ is the Word of God speaking for God's purpose (Rev. 19:13). When He comes to fight God's
enemies for the kingdom, His name is called the Word of God. In
His fighting He is God's speaking. (*Crystallization-study of the
Gospel of John,* p. 16)

Christ's speaking to us surely follows His speaking to the
Father. In other words, His intercession takes place first; then by
His speaking to us He continues to accomplish what He has
interceded.

How busy Christ is! He is not only walking in the midst of the
churches; He is also carrying on His twofold speaking, a Godward
speaking and an usward speaking. He is a walking and a

speaking High Priest....He is both speaking and walking as well....What Christ intercedes for, He then speaks forth to us. Then, after He speaks to us, He again speaks to the Father. He has much to say in Revelation 2 and 3 to the seven churches; correspondingly, He has much to say to the Father for the carrying out of what He has spoken in the seven epistles. This speaking, then, goes back and forth: first to the Father, then to us, then back to the Father again. Hallelujah for our speaking High Priest!

By His walking in the midst of the churches, He gets to know the condition of each church....He traveled through Ephesus, Smyrna, Pergamos, Thyatira, Sardis, Philadelphia, and Laodicea. Such a tour made Him thoroughly familiar with every situation. Then after His seeing, He spoke.

Even today it is the same. Our High Priest in His heavenly ministry is now walking among the churches to look into the condition of each one. Then according to what He sees, He speaks to us. This is the real priestly service. Do not think that what He is saying is doctrine. His speaking is His serving, His ministering. If you reread these seven epistles with this understanding, you will find them altogether new. Many Bible teachers use these epistles to expound doctrines, but what Christ is speaking here is not doctrinal. It is a priestly speaking.

His speaking is according to what He is and also according to the condition of the church. In every epistle He begins by saying who and what He is. Then He also speaks in every case according to what the church is. His speaking is both practical and equipping.

In His walking He is Christ. In His speaking He is the Spirit. At the beginning of each of the seven epistles it is the Lord who speaks (2:1, 8, 12, 18; 3:1, 7, 14). At the end it is the Spirit speaking to the churches (2:7, 11, 17, 29; 3:6, 13, 22)....The walking Christ became the speaking Spirit. (*The Mending Ministry of John,* pp. 119-121, 117-118)

Further Reading: Crystallization-study of the Gospel of John, msg. 1; The Mending Ministry of John, ch. 13

Enlightenment and inspiration: _____

_____
_____
_____

Morning Nourishment

Exo. And Aaron...every morning when he dresses the
30:7 lamps...
27:20 And you shall command the children of Israel to
bring to you pure oil of beaten olives for the light,
to make the lamps burn continually.

What is the nature of this priestly speaking? In the Old Testament there was the lampstand in the tabernacle. Every morning these lamps were trimmed by having their charred wicks snuffed (Exo. 30:7). In addition, they were kept supplied with oil (27:20). To trim is to cut off the charred ends which would no longer burn brightly; to add oil is to supply what is needed. In Revelation 2 and 3 our High Priest was trimming the seven lampstands. He was cutting away those things which were not needed and which frustrated the shining. At the same time He was supplying the oil which was needed and which would make the lampstands burn brightly.

Of all the things He trimmed away, to me the most striking is the synagogue of Satan (Rev. 2:9)....A synagogue is the symbol of Judaism....During the church dispensation this symbol of Judaism became the synagogue of Satan. It is utilized by him in rebellion against God's New Testament economy.

What can we learn from this? Our old religious concepts are against God's economy and need to be trimmed away. These concepts are black, charred, and dark. They are one of the things which hinder the shining of the local churches. Thus, we need our High Priest to step in and trim them away. (*The Mending Ministry of John,* pp. 121-122)

Today's Reading

Today's Christianity has already been Judaized....There are many essential differences between Judaism and the church. Here I wish to mention four points to which we must give special attention: the temple, the law, the priests, and the promises. As their place of worship, the Jews built a splendid temple on this earth of stone and gold. As their standard of behavior, they have the Ten Commandments and many other regulations. In order to attend to spiritual affairs, they have the office of the priests, a group of special people. Finally, they also have the blessings by which they may prosper on this earth. Please notice that Judaism is an earthly religion on this earth.

The special feature of the church is that your body is the dwelling place of God. Individually speaking, every one of us is the temple of God. Corporately speaking, God builds us up and fits us together to become His dwelling place [Eph. 2:21-22]. There is no place of worship in the church; the place of worship is the worshipper. We carry our place of worship wherever we go. This is basically different from Judaism. The temple in Judaism is a material temple; the temple in the church is a spiritual temple....In the church God dwells in man; in Judaism God dwells in a house. Man thinks that he needs a place in order to worship God. Some even call the building the "church." This is Judaism, not the church! The word *church* in Greek is *ekklesia*, which means "the called-out ones." The church is a people bought with the precious blood; this is the church.

The Jews also have laws and regulations for their daily life (God only uses the law to make men know their sins). Whoever is a Jew must keep the Ten Commandments. But the Lord Jesus says clearly that even if you have kept the Ten Commandments, you still lack one thing (Luke 18:20-22). Judaism has a standard of principles for daily living which is written on tablets of stone....In the church there is no law; rather, its law is in another place. It is not written on tablets of stone but on tablets of the heart. The law of the Spirit of life is within us. The Holy Spirit dwells in us; the Holy Spirit is our law....Right or wrong is not on tablets of stone but in the heart [cf. Heb. 8:10; Jer. 31:33]. Today our special feature is that the Spirit of God dwells in us. (*CWWN*, vol. 47, pp. 27, 24-26)

Further Reading: CWWN, vol. 47, "The Orthodoxy of the Church," ch. 3; *Crystallization-study Outlines—Revelation (2),* pp. 18-21

Enlightenment and inspiration: _____

_____

_____

_____

Morning Nourishment

Rev. I know where you dwell, where Satan's throne is...
2:13-15 But I have a few things against you, that you have
some there who hold the teaching of Balaam, who
taught Balak to put a stumbling block before the sons
of Israel, to eat idol sacrifices and to commit fornication. In the same way you also have some who hold in
like manner the teaching of the Nicolaitans.

Another thing which chars the wick is worldliness. This our
heavenly High Priest cannot tolerate. Pergamos (Rev. 2:12-17)
speaks of the marriage of the church with the world. The Lord
again steps in to trim the wick. You who live in New York are
surely living in a worldly city. Apart from the church, I certainly would not like to live here....We may think that those
who live in the countryside are spared from worldliness, but
this is not the case. The country has its worldliness too. All this
worldliness, symbolized by Pergamos, must be trimmed away.
(*The Mending Ministry of John,* p. 122)

Today's Reading

The Greek word [*Pergamos*] means *marriage* (implying union)
and *fortified tower.* As a sign, the church in Pergamos prefigures
the church that entered into a marriage union with the world
and became a high fortified tower, equivalent to the great tree
prophesied by the Lord in the parable of the mustard seed (Matt.
13:31-32). When Satan failed to destroy the church through the
persecution of the Roman Empire in the first three centuries, he
changed his strategy. He sought instead to corrupt her through
Constantine's welcoming of Christianity as the state religion in
the first part of the fourth century. Through Constantine's encouragement and political influence, multitudes of unbelievers
were baptized into the "church," and the "church" became mon-
strously great. Since the church as a chaste bride is espoused to
Christ, her union with the world is considered spiritual fornication in the eyes of God. (Rev. 2:12, footnote 1)

Satan's throne is in the world, the place where he dwells and the sphere of his reign. Since the worldly church entered into union with the world, she dwells where Satan dwells. (Rev. 2:13, footnote 1)

The worldly and degraded church holds not only the teaching of Balaam but also the teaching of the Nicolaitans. The teaching of Balaam distracts believers from the person of Christ to idolatry and from the enjoyment of Christ to spiritual fornication, whereas the teaching of the Nicolaitans destroys the function of believers as members of the Body of Christ, thus annulling the Lord's Body as His expression. The former teaching disregards the Head, and the latter destroys the Body. This is the subtle intention of the enemy in all religious teachings.

In the church in Ephesus only the works of the Nicolaitans were found (Rev. 2:6), whereas in the church in Pergamos their works had progressed to become a teaching. First, the Nicolaitans practiced the hierarchy in the initial church; then they taught it in the degraded church. Today, in both Catholicism and Protestantism, this Nicolaitan hierarchy prevails in both practice and teaching. (Rev. 2:15, footnote 1)

Manna is a type of Christ as the heavenly food that enables God's people to go His way. A portion of manna was preserved in a golden pot concealed in the Ark (Exo. 16:32-34; Heb. 9:4). The open manna was for the Lord's people to enjoy in a public way; the hidden manna, signifying the hidden Christ, is a special portion reserved for His overcoming seekers, who overcome the degradation of the worldly church. While the church goes the way of the world, these overcomers come forward to abide in the presence of God in the Holy of Holies, where they enjoy the hidden Christ as a special portion for their daily supply....If we seek the Lord, overcome the degradation of the worldly church, and enjoy a special portion of the Lord today, He as the hidden manna will be a reward to us in the coming kingdom. If we miss Him as our special portion today in the church life, we will surely lose the enjoyment of Him as a reward in the coming kingdom. (Rev. 2:17, footnote 2)

Further Reading: The Mending Ministry of John, ch. 14

Enlightenment and inspiration: _____

_____

_____

_____

Morning Nourishment

Matt. ...The kingdom of the heavens is like leaven, which
13:33 a woman took and hid in three measures of meal
until the whole was leavened.
Rev. But I have *something* against you, that you toler-
2:20 ate the woman Jezebel, she who calls herself a
prophetess and teaches and leads My slaves astray
to commit fornication and to eat idol sacrifices.
18:2 ...Fallen, fallen is Babylon the Great!...

When the Lord comes to the church in Thyatira, He con-
demns them for tolerating the woman Jezebel (Rev. 2:20). Who
is this evil woman He calls Jezebel? It is the Roman Catholic
Church....The Catholic Church is full of evil. The woman Jezebel is in the church. All that she represents must be trimmed
away. (*The Mending Ministry of John,* pp. 122-123)

The woman here is the same as the one prophesied by the
Lord in Matthew 13:33. There the woman added leaven (signifying evil, heretical, and pagan things) into the fine flour (signifying Christ as the meal offering for the satisfaction of God and
man). This woman is the great harlot of Revelation 17, who mixes
abominations with the divine things. Jezebel, the pagan wife of
Ahab, is a type of this apostate church. (Rev. 2:20, footnote 1)

Today's Reading

[In Matthew 13:33] this woman is Roman Catholicism, the
degraded church. She began to exercise her self-assumed authority....The Bible forbids the church to teach. In typology the
church has no authority to teach. The principle of forbidding the
woman to teach shows us that the church has no authority to
teach. Here the woman began to put leaven into the meal. This
means that the woman began to exercise her authority....The
symbol of the woman means that the church rather than the
Lord is now making all the decisions. It is Jezebel, the prophetess, who is teaching, not the Lord. It would have been better for
the church if it had received its teaching from the Head instead
of assuming the role of teacher for itself. When the church

assumes this role, it results in all kinds of heresies being introduced into the church....Roman Catholicism does not ask men
to take the leaven; it only asks men to take the fine flour which
contains the leaven. Roman Catholicism gives us heresies as
well as truths. It believes that Christ is the Son of God and that
the Lord Jesus died on the cross to accomplish redemption.
These two basic tenets of faith are there, but the fine flour has
been leavened. (*CWWN,* vol. 50, pp. 794, 796)

God hates the principle of Babylon more than anything else.
We must note in His presence how much of our being is still not
absolute for Him. Anything which is halfway and not absolute is
called Babylon. We need God to enlighten us so that in His light
we may judge everything in us which is not absolute toward
Him. Only when we judge ourselves in this way can we confess
that we too hate the principle of Babylon. By His grace, may the
Lord not allow us to seek any glory and honor outside of Christ.

The harlot spoken of in Revelation 17 and 18 is Babylon,
whose deeds are extremely displeasing to God. Why is her con-
duct such an offense to God?...The name *Babylon* originates
from "Babel."...The principle of the tower of Babel involves the
attempt to build up something from earth to reach unto heaven.
When men built this tower, they used bricks....Stone is made by
God, and bricks are made by man. Bricks are a human inven-
tion, a human product. The meaning of Babylon relates to man's
own efforts to build a tower to reach unto heaven. Babylon represents man's ability. It represents a false Christianity, a Christianity which does not allow the Holy Spirit to have authority. It
does not seek the Holy Spirit's guidance; it does all things by
human effort. Everything consists of bricks baked by man;
everything depends upon man's action.

God, however, can never accept this....These things are
man's endeavors to build something from earth to heaven by
human ability, by bricks. (*CWWN,* vol. 34, pp. 105-106, 101-102)

Further Reading: CWWN, vol. 50, ch. 45; vol. 34, ch. 5

Enlightenment and inspiration: _____
_____
_____
_____

Morning Nourishment

Rev. And He cried with a strong voice, saying, Fallen, fall-
18:2 en is Babylon the Great! And she has become a dwelling place of demons and a hold of every unclean
spirit and a hold of every unclean and hateful bird.

7 As much as she has glorified herself and lived luxuriously, as much torment and sorrow give to her;
for she says in her heart, I sit a queen, and I am not
a widow, and I shall by no means see sorrow.

The principle of Babylon…is hypocrisy. There is no reality, yet
people act as if there is in order to obtain glory from man. Here is
a real danger to God's children—pretending to be spiritual. There
is a great deal of spiritual behavior which is acted out in falsehood. It is put on as a veneer. Many long prayers are counterfeit;
many prayerful tones are unreal. There is no reality, but it is
made to appear as if there is. This is the principle of Babylon.

This is entirely opposite from the attitude of the bride. Everything done in falsehood is done in the principle of the harlot, not in
the principle of the bride. It is a great matter for God's children to
be delivered from pretending before man. The principle of Babylon is to pretend in order to receive glory from man. If we set our
sight upon man's glory and man's position in the church, we are
participating in the sin of the Babylonian garment and the sin
committed by Ananias and Sapphira. False consecration is sin,
and false spirituality is also sin. True worship is in spirit and
truthfulness. May God make us true men. (*CWWN,* vol. 34, p. 103)

Today's Reading

In Revelation 18:7…[Babylon] sits as a queen. She has lost
all of her character of being a widow. She has no feeling about
the Lord Jesus being killed and crucified on the cross. Rather,
she says, "I sit a queen." She has lost her faithfulness; she has
missed her proper goal. This is the principle of Babylon, and this
is corrupted Christianity.

Chapter 18 shows us many other things about Babylon, especially regarding the luxuries she enjoyed.…Regardless of whether

it is clothing, food, or housing, if it is excessive or beyond our need, it is luxury and in the principle of Babylon. God allows all that we need, but He does not permit things which are beyond our necessity. We should order our living according to the principle of need; then God will bless us. (*CWWN,* vol. 34, pp. 103-104)

In the last epistle, the one to Laodicea, there is lukewarmness (Rev. 3:15-16)....Lukewarmness also must be trimmed away....[You may be] indifferent, yet still you come to the meetings. You may even be proud that you are moderate, and think, "I'm a middle-of-the-road person. It's good not to be too wild or too committed. I'm not cold, but I'm not hot either."...But we have to be hot! We need to burn others!...Lukewarmness must be trimmed away, along with religion, worldliness, and the evils of Jezebel. Morning by morning the priests did this trimming work. (*The Mending Ministry of John,* p. 123)

Laodicea is a distorted Philadelphia. When brotherly love is gone, Philadelphia immediately turns into the opinions of many. This is the meaning of the word *Laodicea.*

Revelation 3:15 says, "I know your works, that you are neither cold nor hot; I wish that you were cold or hot." This is the characteristic of Laodicea. Verse 17 says, "Because you say, I am wealthy and have become rich and have need of nothing, and do not know that you are wretched and miserable and poor and blind and naked." These are the characteristics of Laodicea. In the eyes of the Lord, the characteristics of Laodicea are lukewarmness and spiritual pride. It is bad enough for it to say, "I am wealthy," but it continues, saying, "and have become rich." The two statements are evil enough, yet it goes on to say that it has "need of nothing."...Where does spiritual pride come from? It comes from history. Some were once rich, and they think that they are still rich. The Lord was once merciful to them, and they remember their history. But now they have lost that reality. (*CWWN,* vol. 50, pp. 784-785)

Further Reading: CWWN, vol. 50, ch. 45

Enlightenment and inspiration: _____
_____
_____
_____

Morning Nourishment

Rev.   **So, because you are lukewarm and neither hot nor**
3:16 **cold, I am about to spew you out of My mouth.**
  2:7 **He who has an ear, let him hear what the Spirit**
     says to the churches. To him who overcomes, to
     him I will give to eat of the tree of life, which is in
     the Paradise of God.
Matt. **But the prudent took oil in their vessels with their**
25:4 **lamps.**

If you want to continue in the way of Philadelphia, remember to humble yourselves before God....God's blessing is with us, but we must be careful when we say this. As soon as we are not careful, we have the flavor of Laodicea: "We are wealthy and have become rich and have need of nothing."

Please bear in mind that we have nothing that we have not received. Those around us may be full of death, but we do not need to be conscious of the fact that we are full of life. Those around us may be poor, but we do not need to be conscious of the fact that we are rich. Those who live before the Lord will not be conscious of their own riches. May the Lord be merciful to us that we may learn to live before Him. May we be rich and yet not know that we are rich. It was better for Moses not to know that his face was shining, even though it did shine! Once a person knows himself, he becomes Laodicea, and the result is lukewarmness. Laodicea means to know everything, but in reality to be fervent about nothing. In name it has everything, but it cannot sacrifice its life for anything. It remembers its former glory but forgets its present condition before God. (*CWWN,* vol. 50, pp. 785-786)

Today's Reading

[The priests] also filled the lamps with oil. What is this infilling? The Lord Jesus said to the church in Ephesus, "To him who overcomes, to him I will give to eat of the tree of life..." (Rev. 2:7). To eat of the tree of life is the best infilling!

Then in Revelation 2:17 He promises the one who overcomes in Pergamos, "To him I will give of the hidden manna." To eat of the hidden manna is to be filled and supplied.

To the church in Laodicea He says, "Behold, I stand at the door and knock; if anyone hears My voice and opens the door, then I will come in to him and dine with him and he with Me" (3:20). By feasting with the Lord, the infilling takes place.

To eat of the tree of life, to eat of the hidden manna, to feast with the Lord: these are all the infilling.

This is Christ's high priestly service. By it all the dark, black things of religion, worldliness, evil, and lukewarmness are trimmed away. Also by it the heavenly, divine element of the tree of life, the hidden manna, and the heavenly feast is ministered to you.

The effect of this heavenly ministry is a metabolic transformation. The old things will be discharged and replaced with something new, heavenly, and divine. You will be transformed into precious stones for the building of God's dwelling place....This ministry is under the heavenly priesthood of Christ. It seeks to trim the churches and supply them with the infilling that all the saints in the churches might be metabolically and organically transformed.

All His service and care has the aim of making you an overcomer. Religion, worldliness, evil things, and lukewarmness are not part of the golden lampstand. But when you eat of the tree of life, when you partake of the hidden manna, and when you enjoy the heavenly feast, this nourishment will become the divine element of which the lampstand is composed. Thus every local church will be a lampstand, and in every local church will be overcomers. These overcomers will make up the lampstand. With them religion, worldliness, evil, and lukewarmness will have been trimmed away. The heavenly element will have been supplied to you as the tree of life, the hidden manna, and the heavenly feast. What you will have is the Triune God Himself. He will become your constituent. With such a golden constitution there will be the lampstand. A lampstand eventually is the overcomers in a local church. (*The Mending Ministry of John,* pp. 124-125)

Further Reading: The Mending Ministry of John, ch. 16

Enlightenment and inspiration: _____

_____

_____

_____

Hymns, #1130

1   Sing praise to Christ Who lives in us,
    The God of our salvation;
    Who saves us by His life divine,
    And not by regulation;
    After we've worked—done all we can,
    His life has power to change a man:
    His life divine can change us.

2   He saves us to the uttermost
    By His life-giving power;
    Transfusing Himself into us,
    He saves us hour by hour.
    He saved the lost by coming in,
    He's saving now from more than sin:
    He's saving us to glory!

3   Our Lord was constituted priest
    To be a real life-giver;
    Life is the nature of this One
    Who can from self deliver:
    His life is indestructible,
    By it He saves us to the full:
    Praise God, He's fully able!

4   His life is fully qualified
    To bring us through to glory;
    Were it not for His tested life,
    'Twould be another story:
    His life was fully tried on earth,
    To crucifixion from His birth:
    He passed through death and Hades.

5   He's pledged to save us to the full,
    His life is operating;
    He's doing everything for us
    'Tis all for our perfecting;
    Our life's a failure at its best,
    Only His life can stand the test:
    His life brings full salvation!

6   He's living now to intercede,
     Continuing forever;
     He undertakes into the age,
     His priesthood changes never;
     He always lives to intercede,
     Such a High Priest is what we need:
     He's higher than the heavens.

7   Come forward now to God through Him,
     Ne'er shrink back to destruction;
     Come forward now to get the life,
     Which brings the proper function;
     Come forward now the life to take,
     By life His people us He'll make,
     And swallow death forever.

Composition for prophecy with main point and sub-points: _____

_____

_____

_____

_____

_____

_____

_____

_____

_____

_____

_____

_____

_____

_____

_____

_____

_____

_____

_____

_____

_____

Eight Aspects of the Church
as the Testimony of Jesus

Scripture Reading: Rev. 19:10; 1:1-2, 10-13; 19:7-9, 14-19; 20:4-6; 21:9, 3, 22

Day 1 **I. The testimony of Jesus (Rev. 19:10) is the seven golden lampstands—divine in nature, shining in darkness, and identical with one another (1:1-2, 10-13; 2:1):**

A. The golden lampstand symbolizes the Triune God—the Father as the substance is embodied in the Son, the Son as the embodiment is expressed through the Spirit, the Spirit is fully realized and expressed as the churches, and the churches are the testimony of Jesus (Exo. 25:31-40; Zech. 4:2-10; Rev. 1:10-12).

B. In the divine thought the golden lampstand is actually a living and growing tree with calyxes and almond blossoms; thus, the lampstand portrays the Triune God embodied in Christ as a living, golden tree of resurrection—growing, branching, budding, and blossoming in us, with us, by us, and out of us as the fruit of the light, which is good in nature, righteous in procedure, and real in expression, so that God may be expressed as reality in our daily walk (Exo. 25:31, 35; Eph. 5:8-9).

C. To experience the golden lampstands as the testimony of Jesus, the corporate expression of Jesus (Acts 9:4-5; 1 Cor. 12:12), we must be filled with the Spirit of Jesus (Acts 16:7) by calling on the name of the Lord Jesus continually (1 Cor. 12:3; Rom. 10:12-13; Lam. 3:55-56) to bear the brands of Jesus (Gal. 6:17) as brothers and fellow partakers in the tribulation, kingdom, and endurance in Jesus (Rev. 1:9-10).

Day 2 **II. The testimony of Jesus is the great multitude** serving God in the temple, the whole Body of God's redeemed, who have been raptured to the heavens to enjoy God's care and the Lamb's shepherding with all the spiritual blessings in the heavenlies and in Christ that can be enjoyed today (7:9-17; Eph. 1:3; Gal. 3:14; Gen. 12:2; cf. Rev. 21:3-4; 22:3-5; Isa. 49:10):

A. The great multitude consists of those who have been purchased by the blood of the Lamb from every nation, tribe, people, and tongue to be the constituents of the church (Rev. 7:9a; 5:9; Rom. 11:25; Acts 15:14, 19; 1 Cor. 6:19-20).

B. The Lamb who is in the midst of the throne will shepherd us and guide us to springs of waters of life (Rev. 7:17a):

1. Shepherding includes feeding; under the shepherding of Christ, "I will lack nothing" (Psa. 23:1).

2. We can never improve ourselves, and we need a shepherd to feed us all the time; He feeds the lambs with His experience as the Lamb of God, who is on the throne of God in and for the house of God (vv. 2-6; Rev. 22:1).

III. The testimony of Jesus is the bright woman, representing the whole Body of God's redeemed, with her man-child, representing the overcomers as the stronger part of God's people (12:1-17):

A. The people of God who produce the overcomers (the man-child) are full of light, showing that God's overcoming people are light-bearers, shining through all generations (vv. 1-5; S. S. 6:10; John 8:12; Matt. 5:14; Prov. 4:18; cf. Gen. 1:16-17).

Day 3   B. The man-child signifies the overcomers who cooperate with Christ to fight against His enemy and usher in God's kingdom (Rev. 12:5-10):

1. The way to become the man-child is for us to be strengthened into the inner man, to be empowered to experience the riches of Christ,

and to be strong through putting on the armor
of God by pray-reading the killing word (Eph.
3:16, 18; 6:10-11, 17-18; Rev. 1:16; 19:13-15).

   2. "They overcame him because of the blood of
      the Lamb and because of the word of their
      testimony, and they loved not their soul-life
      even unto death" (12:11).

IV. **The testimony of Jesus is the firstfruits, signifying the overcomers raptured before the
great tribulation, and the harvest, signifying the majority of the believers raptured at
the end of the great tribulation (14:1-5, 14-16):**

   A. At His first coming to the earth, the Lord sowed
      Himself into His believers; all the believers since
      that time, who have received Him as the seed of
      life, have become God's farm, His crop, on the earth
      (Matt. 13:3-8, 24; 1 Cor. 3:9):

      1. The overcomers as the first ripe ones in God's
         field will be reaped (raptured) before the
         great tribulation to be firstfruits to God
         and to the Lamb (Rev. 14:1-5).

      2. The majority of the believers will ripen
         with the help of the sufferings in the great
         tribulation and will be reaped at the end of
         the great tribulation (v. 15).

   B. The rapture is not mainly for our enjoyment but
      for God's enjoyment; we need to make ourselves
      ready to be raptured not for our happiness but
      for the fulfillment of God's purpose (12:5, 7-11;
      14:1, 4b; 19:7).

   C. The meaning of rapture is to be taken into
      the Lord's presence; in order to be taken into the
      Lord's presence, we must be in His presence
      today (2 Cor. 2:10; 1 John 1:3).

   D. The rapture of the overcomers is for defeating
      the enemy and satisfying God; the Lord needs
      the man-child to fight against His enemy, but
      He needs the firstfruits even more for His satis-
      faction (Rev. 14:1, 4b; cf. S. S. 8:6, 13-14).

Day 4 **V. The testimony of Jesus is the victorious ones standing on the glassy sea, signifying the late overcomers who will pass through the great tribulation and overcome Antichrist and the worshipping of Antichrist (Rev. 15:2-4):**

A. The late overcomers sing the song of Moses (indicating God's triumphant judgment over the enemy of His people) and the song of the Lamb (indicating Christ's redemption experienced by God's people in the presence of their enemy) (v. 3a; Exo. 15:1-18).

B. The late overcomers praise God for His works and His ways, that is, for His acts and His principles; God's ways are righteous in His principles and true in His promises, while His works are great in manifestation and wonderful in nature (Rev. 15:3b-4; Psa. 103:7; cf. 107:10-20).

Day 5 **VI. The testimony of Jesus is the bride of Christ— the overcomers who are the co-kings of Christ during the millennium (Rev. 19:7-9; 20:4, 6):**

A. The Lord's recovery is for the preparation of the bride of Christ (19:7-9; 21:2).

B. Ultimately, we will be conformed to be the wonderful Shulammite, who, as the duplication of Solomon, is the greatest and ultimate figure of the New Jerusalem as the counterpart, the bride, of Christ (S. S. 6:13; Rev. 21:2, 9-10; 22:17a).

C. The Shulammite is likened to the dance of two camps, or two armies (Heb. *mahanaim*), in the sight of God; after Jacob saw the angels of God, the two armies of God, he named the place where he was Mahanaim and divided his wives, children, and possessions into "two armies" (S. S. 6:13; Gen. 32:2):

1. The spiritual significance of the two armies is the strong testimony that we more than conquer, we "super-overcome," through Him who loved us, according to the principle of the

Body of Christ (Rom. 8:37; 12:5; Deut. 32:30; Eccl. 4:9-12).

2. God does not want those who are strong in themselves; He wants only the feeble ones, the weaker ones, the women and children; those who are counted worthy to be over-comers will be the weaker ones who depend on the Lord (1 Cor. 1:26-28; 2 Cor. 12:9-10; 13:3-5; S. S. 8:6).

Day 6 **VII. The testimony of Jesus is the bridal army, who fights together with Christ, the em-bodiment of God, to defeat Antichrist, the embodiment of Satan, with his armies (Rev. 19:14-19; 17:14):**

A. In Ephesians 5 and 6 we see the church as the bride and the warrior; in Revelation 19 we also have these two aspects of the church (Eph. 5:25-27; 6:10-20; Rev. 19:7-9, 11-16):

1. Before Christ descends to earth to deal with Antichrist and the totality of human gov-ernment, He will have a wedding, uniting His overcomers (who have been fighting the battle against God's enemy for years) to Himself as one entity (vv. 7-9; cf. Dan. 7:25; 6:10; Eph. 6:12).

2. After His wedding Christ will come with His newly married bride to destroy Anti-christ, who with his army will fight against God directly (Rev. 19:11-16).

B. In Ephesians 5 the word is for the nourishment that leads to the beautifying of the bride for God's expression, and in Ephesians 6 the word is for the killing that enables the church as the corporate warrior to engage in spiritual warfare for God's dominion, thus fulfilling God's original intention (5:26-27; 6:17-18; Gen. 1:26).

VIII. Ultimately, the testimony of Jesus is the New Jerusalem as the ultimate consummation of the tabernacle and temple—the eternal

divine-human incorporation, the eternal building, of God and man (Rev. 21:9, 3, 22):

A. We can live out and work out the New Jerusalem as the divine-human incorporation by taking the Lord as our abode for us to be His abode (John 15:4-5):

　1. When we love the Lord Jesus, He manifests Himself to us, and the Father comes with Him to make an abode with us for our enjoyment; this abode is a mutual abode, in which the Triune God abides in us and we abide in Him (14:23).

　2. We abide in Christ that He may abide in us by dealing with the constant word in the Scriptures that is outside of us and the present word as the Spirit within us; when we abide in the Lord and let His words abide in us, we are one with Him in actuality (5:39-40; 6:63; 2 Cor. 3:6; Rev. 2:7; John 8:31; 15:7).

B. The overcoming believers as the constituents of God's building, the New Jerusalem, are signified by jasper and other precious stones (Rev. 21:9-11, 18-21; 1 Cor. 3:12a):

　1. Jasper signifies the appearance of God shining with the glory of God as the light of the New Jerusalem for the expression of God (Rev. 4:3; 21:11, 18-19).

　2. The other precious stones signify the riches of the beauty of Christ in different aspects for the foundation of God's eternal dwelling (vv. 19-21).

　3. By the judging Spirit, the burning Spirit, and the flowing Spirit—the Lord Spirit—we are being transformed by the experiences of the riches of Christ as the God of resurrection gained through sufferings, consuming pressures, and the killing work of the cross (Isa. 4:4; 11:2; John 4:14b; 2 Cor. 1:8-9).

4. By our growth in the divine life in Christ as the living stone, we are being transformed into precious stones; through the process of transformation, the Triune God is being wrought into and structured together with us to the praise of the glory of His grace with which He graced us in the Beloved for us to become the New Jerusalem as the ultimate testimony of Jesus and the good news to the entire universe (1 Pet. 2:4; Rev. 21:18-21; Eph. 1:3-6; cf. Luke 4:18-19).

Morning Nourishment

Rev. ...John, who testified the word of God and the tes-
1:1-2 timony of Jesus Christ, *even* all that he saw.
11-12 ...What you see write in a scroll and send *it* to the
seven churches: to Ephesus and to Smyrna and to
Pergamos and to Thyatira and to Sardis and to
Philadelphia and to Laodicea. And I turned to see
the voice that spoke with me; and when I turned, I
saw seven golden lampstands.

The book of Revelation reveals eight aspects of the church as
the testimony of Jesus. The first aspect, in chapters 1 through 3,
is the seven golden lampstands. The lampstands themselves
have three main significances. First, the lampstands shine in
the dark night. Second, the lampstands are golden. In typology,
gold signifies the divine nature....Third, the shining of the
golden lampstands is so that people may see Christ as the Son of
Man walking in their midst....Today Jesus is walking, acting,
moving, living, working, and saving people in the local churches.
(*The Testimony of Jesus,* p. 101)

Today's Reading

The church is not only universally one but also expressed
locally in many cities. In the whole universe there is only one
Christ, one Spirit, and one church. Why then are there the seven
churches? Because of the need for an expression....If we would
know the church, we must know its substance, existence, and
expression. Substantially, the church, and even all the churches,
are one. In expression, the many churches are the many lampstands....The church is the expression of the Triune God, and this
expression is seen in many localities on the earth....In Revelation 1 there are seven lampstands with forty-nine lamps shining
in the universe. This is the testimony of Jesus....This means
that the church is the expression of the Triune God substantially
and expressively. Substantially, it is of one substance in the whole
universe; expressively, it is many lampstands with the lamps
shining in the darkness to express the Triune God. The Father

as the substance is embodied in the Son, the Son as the embodiment is expressed through the Spirit, the Spirit is fully realized and reproduced as the churches, and the churches are the testimony of Jesus. If we see this vision, it will govern us and we shall never be divisive. (*Life-study of Revelation,* p. 92)

[In Exodus 25:31-40 we] see that on [the lampstand] there are twenty-five calyxes. There are three on each branch, three holding one pair of branches each, and four on the shaft of the lampstand, making a total of twenty-five. Since the three calyxes which each hold one pair of branches do not have blossoms, the lampstand has a total of twenty-two blossoms. The divine thought here is that the lampstand is actually a tree with calyxes and blossoms.

Furthermore, the lampstand is described in such a way as to give the idea of growth. These verses speak of branches, buds, and almond blossoms. Blossoming indicates growth. Thus, we must be impressed that the lampstand is a growing tree. As a tree, the lampstand has certain outstanding features. First, it is a golden tree. Gold signifies the nature of God....The golden lampstand is the expression of the Triune God. The Triune God is a living tree, growing, budding, and blossoming.

This golden tree has many almond blossoms. In typology almonds signify resurrection life. Aaron's rod budding with almonds signifies resurrection life. Hence, the almonds on the lampstand indicate that it is a tree in resurrection. Resurrection is life that overcomes death without being damaged or injured by death. Death is powerless to do anything with resurrection life. Death can inflict all kinds of damage on other forms of life, plant life, animal life, and human life. Only one kind of life cannot be hurt by death, and this is resurrection life. Resurrection is life which passes through death and can never be held by it. According to the full revelation of the Scriptures, God Himself is this resurrection life. (*Life-study of Exodus,* pp. 1081-1083)

Further Reading: Life-study of Revelation, msg. 8; *Life-study of Exodus,* msg. 93

Enlightenment and inspiration: _____

_____
_____
_____

Morning Nourishment

Rev. After these things I saw, and behold, *there was* a great
7:9 multitude which no one could number, out of every
nation and *all* tribes and peoples and tongues, standing before the throne and before the Lamb, clothed in
white robes and palm branches in their hands.
17 ...The Lamb who is in the midst of the throne will shepherd them and guide them to springs of waters of life;
and God will wipe away every tear from their eyes.

In Revelation 7:9-17 we see the testimony of Jesus as a great
multitude....Verse 14 says, "These are those who come out of the
great tribulation." This refers to the tribulations, sufferings, per-
secutions, and afflictions experienced by God's redeemed people
throughout the ages. Because the world always afflicts the
church (John 16:33), wherever the church is, there will always be
a certain amount of persecution. This great multitude has come
out of tribulation in a victorious way, for they all hold palm
branches, which signify their victory over tribulation. Revelation
7:15 says, "He who sits upon the throne will tabernacle over
them." Eventually, in eternity, God will overshadow them with
Himself as their tabernacle (21:3; cf. John 1:14). This is the des-
tiny of God's redeemed ones. How wonderful this is! (*The Testimony of Jesus*, p. 103)

Today's Reading

The great multitude in Revelation 7:9-17 consists of the redeemed ones from the nations throughout all generations, who
are innumerable and who constitute the church. That they are
standing before the throne indicates that they have been raptured to the heavens, to the presence of God. Thus, the record in
these verses describes in a general way the scene from the time of
the rapture of the believers to their enjoyment in eternity.

The great tribulation here is tribulation in a general sense....
No Christian can avoid these things. In our spirit, we Christians
are a people of enjoyment, but on the physical side, we are a suffering people. However, one day we shall come triumphantly out

of the great tribulation and stand before the Lamb. The palm branches in the hands of the saints signify their victory over tribulation, which they have undergone for the Lord's sake, and they are also a sign of satisfaction gained through being watered (Exo. 15:27). In eternity, the One who sits on the throne will tabernacle over them, overshadowing them with Himself as the One who is embodied in Christ (John 1:14). Moreover, they will not hunger or thirst any more, for the Lamb who is in the midst of the throne will shepherd them and guide them to springs of waters of life.

Following this, Revelation 12 reveals the third aspect of the testimony of Jesus. Here the figure is not a lampstand but a wonderful, universal, heavenly woman (vv. 1-2, 5-6). Whereas the lampstands are in the dark night, the woman is full of light. With her there is no distinction between day and night, because she is clothed with the sun, the moon is underneath her feet, and on her head is a crown of stars. There is no need for the woman to shine in the darkness, as the lampstands do, because she is always fully in the light. When we come to the lampstands, we are under the shining, and when we come to the woman, we are under the sun, the moon, and the stars. The sun, the moon, and the stars are all heavenly (Gen. 1:16-17). Thus, the woman indicates the heavenly nature, position, and disposition of the church as the testimony of Jesus. With her there is nothing earthly, such as casinos, department stores, television, sports, synagogues, cathedrals, or chapels. Everything about this woman is heavenly.

As long as we are earthly, we are qualified to be food for Satan [3:14]. However, there is no serpent on the sun, the moon, or the stars. The position of the church in the spiritual warfare is not on the earth but in the heavenlies (Eph. 2:6; 6:12). When the church is in the heavenlies, Satan is under her feet. Eventually, Satan is cast down and defeated by the man-child of the wonderful heavenly woman (Rev. 12:10-11). (*The Testimony of Jesus,* pp. 135-136, 103-104)

Further Reading: The Testimony of Jesus, ch. 9

Enlightenment and inspiration: _____
_____
_____
_____

Morning Nourishment

Rev. **And a great sign was seen in heaven: a woman**
12:1 **clothed with the sun, and the moon underneath**
her feet, and on her head a crown of twelve stars.
5 **And she brought forth a son, a man-child, who is to**
shepherd all the nations with an iron rod; and her
child was caught up to God and to His throne.

The wonderful, bright woman [in Revelation 12] has no covering, shadow, or darkness. Everything is in the bright open air. This
kind of church is a victorious one. In this sense, there is no need
for the church to fight against Satan; Satan is already defeated
and cast down, and the kingdom of Christ is brought in. This
woman is heavenly, bright, frank, and thoroughly crystal clear. It
is from such a wonderful church that the man-child is brought
forth (v. 5a). This woman is the third aspect of the church as the
testimony of Jesus. (*The Testimony of Jesus,* pp. 105-106)

Today's Reading

The man-child is the stronger part of the people of God.
Among the people of God, even among those in the Lord's recovery
today, there is the stronger part. The woman will be left on earth
to pass through the great tribulation, but the stronger part, the
man-child, will be raptured to the throne of God before the tribulation (Rev. 12:5b-6). The man-child will be raptured prior to the
tribulation because God needs the man-child to fight against
Satan in the heavens and cast him down to the earth (v. 9).
Although God has many angels who will fight against Satan, the
final victory over the enemy will be gained not because of the
angels but because of the man-child. God needs the man-child.
God will shame Satan by using the very man Satan corrupted to
defeat him....The man-child will fight up to the throne to cast
Satan down from the heavens to the earth. Although Jesus has
defeated Satan on the cross, there is still the need for the church
to execute His victory over the enemy. Because many members of
the Body have failed in this matter, only the stronger part of the
Body, the man-child, will execute Christ's victory over Satan. The

man-child will be raptured to the heavens to accomplish this job.

The rapture is not mainly for our own blessing....We must realize that God has a need for us to be raptured; we must be raptured to heaven to fight against the enemy....If anyone does not go to heaven to meet Satan and cast him down, Satan will come down to the earth to meet and overcome him. We must be the man-child.

The fourth aspect of the church as the testimony of Jesus is that it is God's farm to grow the divine crop. This crop is first the one hundred forty-four thousand firstfruits, a small number, and then the harvest, the majority (14:1-5, 14-16). This tells us that in the church life we all need to grow. Verse 4 shows the way to grow. This verse says concerning the firstfruits, "These are they who have not been defiled with women, for they are virgins. These are they who follow the Lamb wherever He may go." In order to grow, we need to stay away from any kind of defilement. Daniel and his three friends were offered the best food by the royal palace in Babylon, but Daniel purposed in his heart not to defile himself by eating food that had been offered to idols. In this way, these young men kept themselves from being defiled (Dan. 1:5-6, 8)....Young people especially must be careful not to be defiled, and they must also follow Jesus wherever He goes....If the young people will do this and separate themselves to the Lord, they will grow every day, and they will be the firstfruits produced by the church life.

The church is also a farm to grow Christ (1 Cor. 3:9)....Something within us is growing, because the church is God's farm. Some on this farm will be the firstfruits. They will ripen first because they are growing more quickly. They are not defiled, and they follow the Lamb wherever He goes (Rev. 14:4). The condition for growing quickly is to follow the Lamb. Wherever He goes, we follow Him, and by following Him we grow more quickly. Then we will be the firstfruits. Nevertheless, even those who grow more slowly will still ripen to be the harvest. (*The Testimony of Jesus,* pp. 106-107, 137-138)

Further Reading: The Testimony of Jesus, ch. 11

Enlightenment and inspiration: _____

_____

_____

_____

Morning Nourishment

Rev. **And I saw as it were a glassy sea mingled with fire**
15:2-3 **and those who come away victorious from the beast**
and from his image and from the number of his name
standing on the glassy sea, having harps of God. And
they sing the song of Moses, the slave of God, and the
song of the Lamb, saying, Great and wonderful are
Your works, Lord God the Almighty! Righteous and
true are Your ways, O King of the nations!

Revelation 15:2-5 reveals the fifth aspect of the testimony of Jesus—the overcomers standing on a glassy sea mingled with fire before God's heavenly temple. A number of the saints are on the shore of this sea, singing the song of Moses and the song of the Lamb. This is a picture signifying further spiritual matters concerning the testimony of Jesus. The church as the testimony of Jesus is composed of a group of saints who have been saved through water, just as Noah was saved from his evil generation through the water that flooded the earth (Gen. 6:11-14a) and as the Israelites were saved through the water of the Red Sea not only from God's judgment but also from the evil power of Pharaoh (Exo. 14:22, 29)....The flood for Noah and the Red Sea for the Israelites were both a baptism (1 Pet. 3:20-21; 1 Cor. 10:1-2). Today we, the New Testament believers, are also baptized. The real meaning of baptism is that it is a burial (Rom. 6:4). A certain man may be a millionaire with banks, corporations, and many friends and relatives. It will certainly be hard for such a man to break all these ties, but on the day he is buried, he will finally come out of the world. Nothing separates us from all the worldly ties as thoroughly as burial. Anyone who means business with the Lord must see that he has come out of the world by passing through water. (*The Testimony of Jesus,* pp. 108-109)

Today's Reading

In principle, the glassy sea before the throne of God signifies the operation of baptism. Eventually, in Revelation 15 certain of the saved ones are standing on the shore of "baptism," rejoicing and singing just as Israel sang the song of Moses on the shore of the Red Sea.

Revelation 15:2 tells us that the glassy sea is mingled with fire. This sea is not of water but of fire. God's judgment over His fallen creation was firstly with water, but after the flood God told Noah that He would not judge the earth again with water (Gen. 9:15). Instead, from that time onward God's judgment has always been with fire (19:24; Rev. 14:10; 18:8; 19:20; 20:9-10; 21:8). Therefore, the glassy sea mingled with fire signifies both kinds of judgment by God, that by water and that by fire. This glassy sea eventually issues in the lake of fire. In front of the tabernacle was the laver, in front of the temple was the bronze sea with ten lavers, and in front of the heavenly temple there is the glassy sea. Eventually, outside the New Jerusalem there will be the lake of fire where all the things we buried in our baptism will go.

The Israelites were baptized in the Red Sea, but because they had become old and fleshly in the wilderness, they needed to be baptized again in the Jordan. Likewise, we may have been baptized ten years ago, but today we may be full of dirt and old things. We must not bear these things in the church life. In the church there is a glassy sea into which we can jump and be washed. Today the baptistery is an entry for the negative things to go into the lake of fire. We need to let the dirt, the world, and all the negative things pass through that entrance and go into the lake of fire. If we are wearing the modern fashions from the department store, we need the experience of entering into the baptistery to be washed and allow those fashions to go to the lake of fire. Then we will be in the New Jerusalem in our experience. We must not despise the baptistery. It is the best place to send our earthly dirt on the way to the lake of fire....We must not keep the dirt on ourselves. We must be cleansed in the church. (*The Testimony of Jesus,* pp. 109-110)

Further Reading: The Testimony of Jesus, ch. 9

Enlightenment and inspiration: _____
_____
_____
_____

Morning Nourishment

Rev.   ...The marriage of the Lamb has come, and His wife
19:7-8 has made herself ready. And it was given to her that
      she should be clothed in fine linen, bright *and* clean;
      for the fine linen is the righteousnesses of the saints.
S. S. Return, return, O Shulammite; return, return, that
6:13 we may gaze at you. Why should you gaze at the
      Shulammite, as upon the dance of two camps?

The sixth aspect [of the testimony of Jesus] is in Revelation 19, where we see the bride prepared for a wedding by being clothed with fine linen, bright and clean (vv. 7-8). The outer court of the tabernacle was also covered with fine linen (Exo. 26:1). Linen signifies the expression of Christ in the righteousnesses of the saints. Today as the testimony of Jesus the church must be clothed with fine linen, being righteous, bright, pure, clean, clear, and without mixture, spot, or any such thing (Eph. 5:26-27). (*The Testimony of Jesus*, p. 111)

Today's Reading

[We will be] conformed, ultimately, to be the wonderful Shulammite, who, as the duplication of Solomon, is the greatest and ultimate figure of the New Jerusalem as the counterpart of Christ.

[In Song of Songs 6:13] the Shulammite was like two camps, or armies, in the eyes of God. These two armies are dancing in celebration of their victory....The name *Shulammite* is not mentioned in the beginning of Song of Songs....In this verse the Shulammite is likened to two armies, or camps, dancing.

This phrase *two armies* in Hebrew is *Mahanaim*. This is not a common word; it is a historical name from the Old Testament in Genesis 32:2. Jacob decided to go back to his fathers' land when he could no longer stay with his uncle Laban, to whom he had fled from his brother Esau. By that time he had four wives and many children, servants, flocks, and herds. However, his twin brother Esau was still alive. Jacob was returning with the fear that Esau still wanted to kill him. As he journeyed with his family, there were no strong ones with him. There were only feeble ones, women and children. Jacob was very frightened at the prospect of meeting Esau. On the way "the angels of God met him," and Jacob said, "This is God's camp. So he called the name of that place Mahanaim." (Gen. 32:1-2).

After he saw the two armies of God, Jacob did a marvelous thing. He divided his wives, children, and the rest of his possessions into two groups, or "two armies." He thought that if his brother Esau attacked one group, the other group could escape being slaughtered. This is full of spiritual significance. These two groups are not just the singular *army* of God but "two armies." This means that we are more than conquerors. It also signifies a strong testimony. God does not want "giants." He wants only the feeble ones, the weaker ones, the women and children. They can become His armies because the fighting is not in their hands but in His hands. He needs a people who are one with Him, a people who are submissive to Him, signified by the plaited hair (S. S. 1:11), and obedient to Him with a flexible will, signified by the neck with strings of jewels (v. 10).

Dear saints, when that day comes, all who are strong in themselves will be disqualified. Those who are counted as overcomers will be the weaker ones...who depend on the Lord.

In Revelation 3:8 the Lord said that those in Philadelphia had "a little power."...If we are too able and too full of capacity in doing things, we are finished. Today the Lord is waiting. He is still calling for overcomers. If we say, "Lord, I can't overcome," the Lord will say, "My child, whatever you cannot do, I will do for you. I resist the proud, but I give grace to the humble." This is the principle of two armies (Mahanaim) dancing. Remember that these two armies were composed of Jacob's wives and children. Eventually, none of them fought against Esau. It was God who fought Esau by changing his attitude....Today we are the reality of God's armies (Mahanaim). (*Crystallization-study of Song of Songs,* pp. 9, 110-112)

Further Reading: Crystallization-study of Song of Songs, msgs. 1, 12

Enlightenment and inspiration: _____
_____
_____
_____

Morning Nourishment

Rev. **And the armies which are in heaven followed Him on**
19:14 **white horses, dressed in fine linen, white** *and* **clean.**
21:10-11 **And he...showed me the holy city, Jerusalem, com-**
ing down out of heaven from God, having the glory
of God. Her light was like a most precious stone,
like a jasper stone, as clear as crystal.

The seventh aspect of the testimony of Jesus is the overcoming army to fight against Antichrist. The stronger part of
the church, the man-child who fights against Satan in the heavens, will also be a part of the army that fights with Christ against
Satan on the earth (Rev. 19:14-19)....After all the raptured saints
are judged at the judgment seat of Christ (2 Cor. 5:10), the overcomers will return to the earth with Christ as His heavenly
army to fight against Antichrist with his earthly armies....
Eventually, at the end of this war, Christ will defeat Antichrist
(Rev. 19:20). (*The Testimony of Jesus*, p. 112)

Today's Reading

The eighth aspect of the testimony of Jesus is the New Jerusalem. The wall of the New Jerusalem is built with jasper (Rev. 21:11,
18-19)....The appearance of God on the throne is like jasper (4:3a).
Therefore, jasper signifies the precious and divine appearance,
likeness, expression, and image of God. That the New Jerusalem
has the appearance of jasper signifies that it is the fulfillment of
Genesis 1:26. Man was made in God's image to express God, and in
the New Jerusalem this purpose will be fulfilled. The entire redeemed human race will express God. The appearance of God is
like jasper, and the New Jerusalem will appear the same. Because
the New Jerusalem is the expression of God, it will be His consummate, corporate testimony. (*The Testimony of Jesus*, pp. 112-113)

The New Jerusalem is a mutual abode. The Triune God in
eternity will abide in His chosen people, and His chosen people
will abide in Him. His chosen people will be His abode, and He
Himself will be their abode. This is why the New Jerusalem, the
holy city,...is a tabernacle for God's dwelling and a temple for

our dwelling, in which we live to serve God. (*Living in and with the Divine Trinity,* p. 102)

We abide in Christ so that He may abide in us by dealing with the constant word in the Scriptures, which is outside of us, and the present word as the Spirit, which is within us (John 5:39-40; 6:63; 2 Cor. 3:6; Rev. 2:7). By the outward, written word we have the explanation, definition, and expression of the mysterious Lord, and by the inward, living word we have the experience of the abiding Christ and the presence of the practical Lord (Eph. 5:26; 6:17-18). If we abide in the Lord's constant and written word, His instant and living words will abide in us (John 8:31; 15:7; 1 John 2:14). We abide in Him and His words abide in us so that we may speak in Him and He may speak in us for the building of God into man and man into God (John 15:7; 2 Cor. 2:17; 13:3; 1 Cor. 14:4b). (*The Conclusion of the New Testament,* p. 3995)

After the millennial kingdom, the New Jerusalem as the totality of all God's chosen and redeemed people will appear. In the thousand years the bride wears fine linen, but in eternity the New Jerusalem will be built with jasper (Rev. 21:18-19). In the Old Testament the tabernacle was covered with white linen. However, this was something temporary, not eternal. After the tabernacle there was the temple, which was built no longer with linen but with precious stones....The final aspect of the testimony of Jesus...will be the New Jerusalem in eternity, expressing God no longer only as white linen but as precious, glowing, shining jasper.

Step after step and aspect after aspect, the testimony of Jesus begins with the lampstands, passes through the great multitude, the universal, bright woman, the firstfruits and harvest, the overcomers on the glassy sea, the bride, and the army, and it finally comes to the New Jerusalem, where Christ is fully expressed and testified. The New Jerusalem will be the testimony of Jesus in the fullest, ultimate way. (*The Testimony of Jesus,* pp. 141-142)

Further Reading: Living in and with the Divine Trinity, ch. 10; *The Conclusion of the New Testament,* msg. 394

Enlightenment and inspiration: _____

_____
_____
_____

Hymns, #1259

1   See the local churches,
   'Midst the earth's dark night;
   Jesus' testimony,
   Bearing Him as light.
   Formed by Him, unmeasured,
   In the Spirit's mold—
   All are one in nature,
   One pure work of gold.

      See the local churches,
      'Midst the earth's dark night;
      Burning in the Spirit,
      Shining forth with Christ.

2   God in Christ, embodied,
   As God's lampstand, He
   Has become the Spirit,
   The reality.
   Spirit as the lampstand
   Has been multiplied;
   Many local churches,
   Now are realized!

3   Caring for the churches
   Is the Son of Man:
   Voice of many waters,
   Stars in His right hand;
   Eyes aflame; His face is
   Shining as the sun;
   Churches—fear no trial,
   He's the living One!

4   What can quench the lampstands?
   Who can them defy?
   More the opposition—
   More they multiply!
   Deeper darkness 'round them,
   Brighter do they shine.
   They are constituted
   With the life divine.

5   Soon the local churches
     Shall the Bride become,
     Bringing in that city—
     New Jerusalem.
     Then the many lampstands
     Shall one lampstand be;
     Triune God expressing,
     Universally.

        Lo, from heav'n descending,
        All the earth shall see
        God's complete expression,
        For eternity.

Composition for prophecy with main point and sub-points: _____

_____

_____

_____

_____

_____

_____

_____

_____

_____

_____

_____

_____

_____

_____

_____

_____

_____

_____

_____

_____

_____

_____

_____

_____

Wk.	Lord's Day	Monday	Tuesday	Wednesday	Thursday	Friday	Saturday
			Reading Schedule for the Recovery Version of the Old Testament with Footnotes				
1	Gen. 1:1-5 ☐	1:6-23 ☐	1:24-31 ☐	2:1-9 ☐	2:10-25 ☐	3:1-13 ☐	3:14-24 ☐
2	4:1-26 ☐	5:1-32 ☐	6:1-22 ☐	7:1—8:3 ☐	8:4-22 ☐	9:1-29 ☐	10:1-32 ☐
3	11:1-32 ☐	12:1-20 ☐	13:1-18 ☐	14:1-24 ☐	15:1-21 ☐	16:1-16 ☐	17:1-27 ☐
4	18:1-33 ☐	19:1-38 ☐	20:1-18 ☐	21:1-34 ☐	22:1-24 ☐	23:1—24:27 ☐	24:28-67 ☐
5	25:1-34 ☐	26:1-35 ☐	27:1-46 ☐	28:1-22 ☐	29:1-35 ☐	30:1-43 ☐	31:1-55 ☐
6	32:1-32 ☐	33:1—34:31 ☐	35:1-29 ☐	36:1-43 ☐	37:1-36 ☐	38:1—39:23 ☐	40:1—41:13 ☐
7	41:14-57 ☐	42:1-38 ☐	43:1-34 ☐	44:1-34 ☐	45:1-28 ☐	46:1-34 ☐	47:1-31 ☐
8	48:1-22 ☐	49:1-15 ☐	49:16-33 ☐	50:1-26 ☐	Exo. 1:1-22 ☐	2:1-25 ☐	3:1-22 ☐
9	4:1-31 ☐	5:1-23 ☐	6:1-30 ☐	7:1-25 ☐	8:1-32 ☐	9:1-35 ☐	10:1-29 ☐
10	11:1-10 ☐	12:1-14 ☐	12:15-36 ☐	12:37-51 ☐	13:1-22 ☐	14:1-31 ☐	15:1-27 ☐
11	16:1-36 ☐	17:1-16 ☐	18:1-27 ☐	19:1-25 ☐	20:1-26 ☐	21:1-36 ☐	22:1-31 ☐
12	23:1-33 ☐	24:1-18 ☐	25:1-22 ☐	25:23-40 ☐	26:1-14 ☐	26:15-37 ☐	27:1-21 ☐
13	28:1-21 ☐	28:22-43 ☐	29:1-21 ☐	29:22-46 ☐	30:1-10 ☐	30:11-38 ☐	31:1-17 ☐
14	31:18—32:35 ☐	33:1-23 ☐	34:1-35 ☐	35:1-35 ☐	36:1-38 ☐	37:1-29 ☐	38:1-31 ☐
15	39:1-43 ☐	40:1-38 ☐	Lev. 1:1-17 ☐	2:1-16 ☐	3:1-17 ☐	4:1-35 ☐	5:1-19 ☐
16	6:1-30 ☐	7:1-38 ☐	8:1-36 ☐	9:1-24 ☐	10:1-20 ☐	11:1-47 ☐	12:1-8 ☐
17	13:1-28 ☐	13:29-59 ☐	14:1-18 ☐	14:19-32 ☐	14:33-57 ☐	15:1-33 ☐	16:1-17 ☐
18	16:18-34 ☐	17:1-16 ☐	18:1-30 ☐	19:1-37 ☐	20:1-27 ☐	21:1-24 ☐	22:1-33 ☐
19	23:1-22 ☐	23:23-44 ☐	24:1-23 ☐	25:1-23 ☐	25:24-55 ☐	26:1-24 ☐	26:25-46 ☐
20	27:1-34 ☐	Num. 1:1-54 ☐	2:1-34 ☐	3:1-51 ☐	4:1-49 ☐	5:1-31 ☐	6:1-27 ☐
21	7:1-41 ☐	7:42-88 ☐	7:89—8:26 ☐	9:1-23 ☐	10:1-36 ☐	11:1-35 ☐	12:1—13:33 ☐
22	14:1-45 ☐	15:1-41 ☐	16:1-50 ☐	17:1—18:7 ☐	18:8-32 ☐	19:1-22 ☐	20:1-29 ☐
23	21:1-35 ☐	22:1-41 ☐	23:1-30 ☐	24:1-25 ☐	25:1-18 ☐	26:1-65 ☐	27:1-23 ☐
24	28:1-31 ☐	29:1-40 ☐	30:1—31:24 ☐	31:25-54 ☐	32:1-42 ☐	33:1-56 ☐	34:1-29 ☐
25	35:1-34 ☐	36:1-13 ☐	Deut. 1:1-46 ☐	2:1-37 ☐	3:1-29 ☐	4:1-49 ☐	5:1-33 ☐
26	6:1—7:26 ☐	8:1-20 ☐	9:1-29 ☐	10:1-22 ☐	11:1-32 ☐	12:1-32 ☐	13:1—14:21 ☐

Reading Schedule for the Recovery Version of the Old Testament with Footnotes

Wk.	Lord's Day	Monday	Tuesday	Wednesday	Thursday	Friday	Saturday
27	14:22—15:23 ☐	16:1-22 ☐	17:1—18:8 ☐	18:9—19:21 ☐	20:1—21:17 ☐	21:18—22:30 ☐	23:1-25 ☐
28	24:1-22 ☐	25:1-19 ☐	26:1-19 ☐	27:1-26 ☐	28:1-68 ☐	29:1-29 ☐	30:1—31:29 ☐
29	31:30—32:52 ☐	33:1-29 ☐	34:1-12 ☐	Josh. 1:1-18 ☐	2:1-24 ☐	3:1-17 ☐	4:1-24 ☐
30	5:1-15 ☐	6:1-27 ☐	7:1-26 ☐	8:1-35 ☐	9:1-27 ☐	10:1-43 ☐	11:1—12:24 ☐
31	13:1-33 ☐	14:1—15:63 ☐	16:1—18:28 ☐	19:1-51 ☐	20:1—21:45 ☐	22:1-34 ☐	23:1—24:33 ☐
32	Judg. 1:1-36 ☐	2:1-23 ☐	3:1-31 ☐	4:1-24 ☐	5:1-31 ☐	6:1-40 ☐	7:1-25 ☐
33	8:1-35 ☐	9:1-57 ☐	10:1—11:40 ☐	12:1—13:25 ☐	14:1—15:20 ☐	16:1-31 ☐	17:1—18:31 ☐
34	19:1-30 ☐	20:1-48 ☐	21:1-25 ☐	Ruth 1:1-22 ☐	2:1-23 ☐	3:1-18 ☐	4:1-22 ☐
35	1 Sam. 1:1-28 ☐	2:1-36 ☐	3:1—4:22 ☐	5:1—6:21 ☐	7:1—8:22 ☐	9:1-27 ☐	10:1—11:15 ☐
36	12:1—13:23 ☐	14:1-52 ☐	15:1-35 ☐	16:1-23 ☐	17:1-58 ☐	18:1-30 ☐	19:1-24 ☐
37	20:1-42 ☐	21:1—22:23 ☐	23:1—24:22 ☐	25:1-44 ☐	26:1-25 ☐	27:1—28:25 ☐	29:1—30:31 ☐
38	31:1-13 ☐	2 Sam. 1:1-27 ☐	2:1-32 ☐	3:1-39 ☐	4:1—5:25 ☐	6:1-23 ☐	7:1-29 ☐
39	8:1—9:13 ☐	10:1—11:27 ☐	12:1-31 ☐	13:1-39 ☐	14:1-33 ☐	15:1—16:23 ☐	17:1—18:33 ☐
40	19:1-43 ☐	20:1—21:22 ☐	22:1-51 ☐	23:1-39 ☐	24:1-25 ☐	1 Kings 1:1-19 ☐	1:20-53 ☐
41	2:1-46 ☐	3:1-28 ☐	4:1-34 ☐	5:1—6:38 ☐	7:1-22 ☐	7:23-51 ☐	8:1-36 ☐
42	8:37-66 ☐	9:1-28 ☐	10:1-29 ☐	11:1-43 ☐	12:1-33 ☐	13:1-34 ☐	14:1-31 ☐
43	15:1-34 ☐	16:1—17:24 ☐	18:1-46 ☐	19:1-21 ☐	20:1-43 ☐	21:1—22:53 ☐	2 Kings 1:1-18 ☐
44	2:1—3:27 ☐	4:1-44 ☐	5:1—6:33 ☐	7:1-20 ☐	8:1-29 ☐	9:1-37 ☐	10:1-36 ☐
45	11:1—12:21 ☐	13:1—14:29 ☐	15:1-38 ☐	16:1-20 ☐	17:1-41 ☐	18:1-37 ☐	19:1-37 ☐
46	20:1—21:26 ☐	22:1-20 ☐	23:1-37 ☐	24:1—25:30 ☐	1 Chron. 1:1-54 ☐	2:1—3:24 ☐	4:1—5:26 ☐
47	6:1-81 ☐	7:1-40 ☐	8:1-40 ☐	9:1-44 ☐	10:1—11:47 ☐	12:1-40 ☐	13:1—14:17 ☐
48	15:1—16:43 ☐	17:1-27 ☐	18:1—19:19 ☐	20:1—21:30 ☐	22:1—23:32 ☐	24:1—25:31 ☐	26:1-32 ☐
49	27:1-34 ☐	28:1—29:30 ☐	2 Chron. 1:1-17 ☐	2:1—3:17 ☐	4:1—5:14 ☐	6:1-42 ☐	7:1—8:18 ☐
50	9:1—10:19 ☐	11:1—12:16 ☐	13:1—15:19 ☐	16:1—17:19 ☐	18:1—19:11 ☐	20:1-37 ☐	21:1—22:12 ☐
51	23:1—24:27 ☐	25:1—26:23 ☐	27:1—28:27 ☐	29:1-36 ☐	30:1—31:21 ☐	32:1-33 ☐	33:1—34:33 ☐
52	35:1—36:23 ☐	Ezra 1:1-11 ☐	2:1-70 ☐	3:1—4:24 ☐	5:1—6:22 ☐	7:1-28 ☐	8:1-36 ☐

Reading Schedule for the Recovery Version of the Old Testament with Footnotes

Wk.	Lord's Day	Monday	Tuesday	Wednesday	Thursday	Friday	Saturday
53	9:1—10:44 ☐	Neh. 1:1-11 ☐	2:1—3:32 ☐	4:1—5:19 ☐	6:1-19 ☐	7:1-73 ☐	8:1-18 ☐
54	9:1-20 ☐	9:21-38 ☐	10:1—11:36 ☐	12:1-47 ☐	13:1-31 ☐	Esth. 1:1-22 ☐	2:1—3:15 ☐
55	4:1—5:14 ☐	6:1—7:10 ☐	8:1-17 ☐	9:1—10:3 ☐	Job 1:1-22 ☐	2:1—3:26 ☐	4:1—5:27 ☐
56	6:1—7:21 ☐	8:1—9:35 ☐	10:1—11:20 ☐	12:1—13:28 ☐	14:1—15:35 ☐	16:1—17:16 ☐	18:1—19:29 ☐
57	20:1—21:34 ☐	22:1—23:17 ☐	24:1—25:6 ☐	26:1—27:23 ☐	28:1—29:25 ☐	30:1—31:40 ☐	32:1—33:33 ☐
58	34:1—35:16 ☐	36:1-33 ☐	37:1-24 ☐	38:1-41 ☐	39:1-30 ☐	40:1-24 ☐	41:1-34 ☐
59	42:1-17 ☐	Psa. 1:1-6 ☐	2:1—3:8 ☐	4:1—6:10 ☐	7:1—8:9 ☐	9:1—10:18 ☐	11:1—15:5 ☐
60	16:1—17:15 ☐	18:1-50 ☐	19:1—21:13 ☐	22:1-31 ☐	23:1—24:10 ☐	25:1—27:14 ☐	28:1—30:12 ☐
61	31:1—32:11 ☐	33:1—34:22 ☐	35:1—36:12 ☐	37:1-40 ☐	38:1—39:13 ☐	40:1—41:13 ☐	42:1—43:5 ☐
62	44:1-26 ☐	45:1-17 ☐	46:1—48:14 ☐	49:1—50:23 ☐	51:1—52:9 ☐	53:1—55:23 ☐	56:1—58:11 ☐
63	59:1—61:8 ☐	62:1—64:10 ☐	65:1—67:7 ☐	68:1-35 ☐	69:1—70:5 ☐	71:1—72:20 ☐	73:1—74:23 ☐
64	75:1—77:20 ☐	78:1-72 ☐	79:1—81:16 ☐	82:1—84:12 ☐	85:1—87:7 ☐	88:1—89:52 ☐	90:1—91:16 ☐
65	92:1—94:23 ☐	95:1—97:12 ☐	98:1—101:8 ☐	102:1—103:22 ☐	104:1—105:45 ☐	106:1-48 ☐	107:1-43 ☐
66	108:1—109:31 ☐	110:1—112:10 ☐	113:1—115:18 ☐	116:1—118:29 ☐	119:1-32 ☐	119:33-72 ☐	119:73-120 ☐
67	119:121-176 ☐	120:1—124:8 ☐	125:1—128:6 ☐	129:1—132:18 ☐	133:1—135:21 ☐	136:1—138:8 ☐	139:1—140:13 ☐
68	141:1—144:15 ☐	145:1—147:20 ☐	148:1—150:6 ☐	Prov. 1:1-33 ☐	2:1—3:35 ☐	4:1—5:23 ☐	6:1-35 ☐
69	7:1—8:36 ☐	9:1—10:32 ☐	11:1—12:28 ☐	13:1—14:35 ☐	15:1-33 ☐	16:1-33 ☐	17:1-28 ☐
70	18:1-24 ☐	19:1—20:30 ☐	21:1—22:29 ☐	23:1-35 ☐	24:1—25:28 ☐	26:1—27:27 ☐	28:1—29:27 ☐
71	30:1-33 ☐	31:1-31 ☐	Eccl. 1:1-18 ☐	2:1—3:22 ☐	4:1—5:20 ☐	6:1—7:29 ☐	8:1—9:18 ☐
72	10:1—11:10 ☐	12:1-14 ☐	S.S. 1:1-8 ☐	1:9-17 ☐	2:1-17 ☐	3:1-11 ☐	4:1-8 ☐
73	4:9-16 ☐	5:1-16 ☐	6:1-13 ☐	7:1-13 ☐	8:1-14 ☐	Isa. 1:1-11 ☐	1:12-31 ☐
74	2:1-22 ☐	3:1-26 ☐	4:1-6 ☐	5:1-30 ☐	6:1-13 ☐	7:1-25 ☐	8:1-22 ☐
75	9:1-21 ☐	10:1-34 ☐	11:1—12:6 ☐	13:1-22 ☐	14:1-14 ☐	14:15-32 ☐	15:1—16:14 ☐
76	17:1—18:7 ☐	19:1-25 ☐	20:1—21:17 ☐	22:1-25 ☐	23:1-18 ☐	24:1-23 ☐	25:1-12 ☐
77	26:1-21 ☐	27:1-13 ☐	28:1-29 ☐	29:1-24 ☐	30:1-33 ☐	31:1—32:20 ☐	33:1-24 ☐
78	34:1-17 ☐	35:1-10 ☐	36:1-22 ☐	37:1-38 ☐	38:1—39:8 ☐	40:1-31 ☐	41:1-29 ☐

Reading Schedule for the Recovery Version of the Old Testament with Footnotes

Wk.	Lord's Day	Monday	Tuesday	Wednesday	Thursday	Friday	Saturday
79	□ 42:1-25	□ 43:1-28	□ 44:1-28	□ 45:1-25	□ 46:1-13	□ 47:1-15	□ 48:1-22
80	□ 49:1-13	□ 49:14-26	□ 50:1—51:23	□ 52:1-15	□ 53:1-12	□ 54:1-17	□ 55:1-13
81	□ 56:1-12	□ 57:1-21	□ 58:1-14	□ 59:1-21	□ 60:1-22	□ 61:1-11	□ 62:1-12
82	□ 63:1-19	□ 64:1-12	□ 65:1-25	□ 66:1-24	□ Jer. 1:1-19	□ 2:1-19	□ 2:20-37
83	□ 3:1-25	□ 4:1-31	□ 5:1-31	□ 6:1-30	□ 7:1-34	□ 8:1-22	□ 9:1-26
84	□ 10:1-25	□ 11:1—12:17	□ 13:1-27	□ 14:1-22	□ 15:1-21	□ 16:1—17:27	□ 18:1-23
85	□ 19:1—20:18	□ 21:1—22:30	□ 23:1-40	□ 24:1—25:38	□ 26:1—27:22	□ 28:1—29:32	□ 30:1-24
86	□ 31:1-23	□ 31:24-40	□ 32:1-44	□ 33:1-26	□ 34:1-22	□ 35:1-19	□ 36:1-32
87	□ 37:1-21	□ 38:1-28	□ 39:1—40:16	□ 41:1—42:22	□ 43:1—44:30	□ 45:1—46:28	□ 47:1—48:16
88	□ 48:17-47	□ 49:1-22	□ 49:23-39	□ 50:1-27	□ 50:28-46	□ 51:1-27	□ 51:28-64
89	□ 52:1-34	□ Lam. 1:1-22	□ 2:1-22	□ 3:1-39	□ 3:40-66	□ 4:1-22	□ 5:1-22
90	□ Ezek. 1:1-14	□ 1:15-28	□ 2:1—3:27	□ 4:1—5:17	□ 6:1—7:27	□ 8:1—9:11	□ 10:1—11:25
91	□ 12:1—13:23	□ 14:1—15:8	□ 16:1-63	□ 17:1—18:32	□ 19:1-14	□ 20:1-49	□ 21:1-32
92	□ 22:1-31	□ 23:1-49	□ 24:1-27	□ 25:1—26:21	□ 27:1-36	□ 28:1-26	□ 29:1—30:26
93	□ 31:1—32:32	□ 33:1-33	□ 34:1-31	□ 35:1—36:21	□ 36:22-38	□ 37:1-28	□ 38:1—39:29
94	□ 40:1-27	□ 40:28-49	□ 41:1-26	□ 42:1—43:27	□ 44:1-31	□ 45:1-25	□ 46:1-24
95	□ 47:1-23	□ 48:1-35	□ Dan. 1:1-21	□ 2:1-30	□ 2:31-49	□ 3:1-30	□ 4:1-37
96	□ 5:1-31	□ 6:1-28	□ 7:1-12	□ 7:13-28	□ 8:1-27	□ 9:1-27	□ 10:1-21
97	□ 11:1-22	□ 11:23-45	□ 12:1-13	□ Hosea 1:1-11	□ 2:1-23	□ 3:1—4:19	□ 5:1-15
98	□ 6:1-11	□ 7:1-16	□ 8:1-14	□ 9:1-17	□ 10:1-15	□ 11:1-12	□ 12:1-14
99	□ 13:1—14:9	□ Joel 1:1-20	□ 2:1-16	□ 2:17-32	□ 3:1-21	□ Amos 1:1-15	□ 2:1-16
100	□ 3:1-15	□ 4:1—5:27	□ 6:1—7:17	□ 8:1—9:15	□ Obad. 1-21	□ Jonah 1:1-17	□ 2:1—4:11
101	□ Micah 1:1-16	□ 2:1—3:12	□ 4:1—5:15	□ 6:1—7:20	□ Nahum 1:1-15	□ 2:1—3:19	□ Hab. 1:1-17
102	□ 2:1-20	□ 3:1-19	□ Zeph. 1:1-18	□ 2:1-15	□ 3:1-20	□ Hag. 1:1-15	□ 2:1-23
103	□ Zech. 1:1-21	□ 2:1-13	□ 3:1-10	□ 4:1-14	□ 5:1—6:15	□ 7:1—8:23	□ 9:1-17
104	□ 10:1—11:17	□ 12:1—13:9	□ 14:1-21	□ Mal. 1:1-14	□ 2:1-17	□ 3:1-18	□ 4:1-6

Reading Schedule for the Recovery Version of the New Testament with Footnotes

Wk.	Lord's Day	Monday	Tuesday	Wednesday	Thursday	Friday	Saturday
1	Matt. 1:1-2 □	1:3-7 □	1:8-17 □	1:18-25 □	2:1-23 □	3:1-6 □	3:7-17 □
2	4:1-11 □	4:12-25 □	5:1-4 □	5:5-12 □	5:13-20 □	5:21-26 □	5:27-48 □
3	6:1-8 □	6:9-18 □	6:19-34 □	7:1-12 □	7:13-29 □	8:1-13 □	8:14-22 □
4	8:23-34 □	9:1-13 □	9:14-17 □	9:18-34 □	9:35—10:5 □	10:6-25 □	10:26-42 □
5	11:1-15 □	11:16-30 □	12:1-14 □	12:15-32 □	12:33-42 □	12:43—13:2 □	13:3-12 □
6	13:13-30 □	13:31-43 □	13:44-58 □	14:1-13 □	14:14-21 □	14:22-36 □	15:1-20 □
7	15:21-31 □	15:32-39 □	16:1-12 □	16:13-20 □	16:21-28 □	17:1-13 □	17:14-27 □
8	18:1-14 □	18:15-22 □	18:23-35 □	19:1-15 □	19:16-30 □	20:1-16 □	20:17-34 □
9	21:1-11 □	21:12-22 □	21:23-32 □	21:33-46 □	22:1-22 □	22:23-33 □	22:34-46 □
10	23:1-12 □	23:13-39 □	24:1-14 □	24:15-31 □	24:32-51 □	25:1-13 □	25:14-30 □
11	25:31-46 □	26:1-16 □	26:17-35 □	26:36-46 □	26:47-64 □	26:65-75 □	27:1-26 □
12	27:27-44 □	27:45-56 □	27:57—28:15 □	28:16-20 □	Mark 1:1 □	1:2-6 □	1:7-13 □
13	1:14-28 □	1:29-45 □	2:1-12 □	2:13-28 □	3:1-19 □	3:20-35 □	4:1-25 □
14	4:26-41 □	5:1-20 □	5:21-43 □	6:1-29 □	6:30-56 □	7:1-23 □	7:24-37 □
15	8:1-26 □	8:27—9:1 □	9:2-29 □	9:30-50 □	10:1-16 □	10:17-34 □	10:35-52 □
16	11:1-16 □	11:17-33 □	12:1-27 □	12:28-44 □	13:1-13 □	13:14-37 □	14:1-26 □
17	14:27-52 □	14:53-72 □	15:1-15 □	15:16-47 □	16:1-8 □	16:9-20 □	Luke 1:1-4 □
18	1:5-25 □	1:26-46 □	1:47-56 □	1:57-80 □	2:1-8 □	2:9-20 □	2:21-39 □
19	2:40-52 □	3:1-20 □	3:21-38 □	4:1-13 □	4:14-30 □	4:31-44 □	5:1-26 □
20	5:27—6:16 □	6:17-38 □	6:39-49 □	7:1-17 □	7:18-23 □	7:24-35 □	7:36-50 □
21	8:1-15 □	8:16-25 □	8:26-39 □	8:40-56 □	9:1-17 □	9:18-26 □	9:27-36 □
22	9:37-50 □	9:51-62 □	10:1-11 □	10:12-24 □	10:25-37 □	10:38-42 □	11:1-13 □
23	11:14-26 □	11:27-36 □	11:37-54 □	12:1-12 □	12:13-21 □	12:22-34 □	12:35-48 □
24	12:49-59 □	13:1-9 □	13:10-17 □	13:18-30 □	13:31—14:6 □	14:7-14 □	14:15-24 □
25	14:25-35 □	15:1-10 □	15:11-21 □	15:22-32 □	16:1-13 □	16:14-22 □	16:23-31 □
26	17:1-19 □	17:20-37 □	18:1-14 □	18:15-30 □	18:31-43 □	19:1-10 □	19:11-27 □

Reading Schedule for the Recovery Version of the New Testament with Footnotes

Wk.	Lord's Day	Monday	Tuesday	Wednesday	Thursday	Friday	Saturday
27	Luke 19:28-48 □	20:1-19 □	20:20-38 □	20:39—21:4 □	21:5-27 □	21:28-38 □	22:1-20 □
28	22:21-38 □	22:39-54 □	22:55-71 □	23:1-43 □	23:44-56 □	24:1-12 □	24:13-35 □
29	24:36-53 □	John 1:1-13 □	1:14-18 □	1:19-34 □	1:35-51 □	2:1-11 □	2:12-22 □
30	2:23—3:13 □	3:14-21 □	3:22-36 □	4:1-14 □	4:15-26 □	4:27-42 □	4:43-54 □
31	5:1-16 □	5:17-30 □	5:31-47 □	6:1-15 □	6:16-31 □	6:32-51 □	6:52-71 □
32	7:1-9 □	7:10-24 □	7:25-36 □	7:37-52 □	7:53—8:11 □	8:12-27 □	8:28-44 □
33	8:45-59 □	9:1-13 □	9:14-34 □	9:35—10:9 □	10:10-30 □	10:31—11:4 □	11:5-22 □
34	11:23-40 □	11:41-57 □	12:1-11 □	12:12-24 □	12:25-36 □	12:37-50 □	13:1-11 □
35	13:12-30 □	13:31-38 □	14:1-6 □	14:7-20 □	14:21-31 □	15:1-11 □	15:12-27 □
36	16:1-15 □	16:16-33 □	17:1-5 □	17:6-13 □	17:14-24 □	17:25—18:11 □	18:12-27 □
37	18:28-40 □	19:1-16 □	19:17-30 □	19:31-42 □	20:1-13 □	20:14-18 □	20:19-22 □
38	20:23-31 □	21:1-14 □	21:15-22 □	21:23-25 □	Acts 1:1-8 □	1:9-14 □	1:15-26 □
39	2:1-13 □	2:14-21 □	2:22-36 □	2:37-41 □	2:42-47 □	3:1-18 □	3:19—4:22 □
40	4:23-37 □	5:1-16 □	5:17-32 □	5:33-42 □	6:1—7:1 □	7:2-29 □	7:30-60 □
41	8:1-13 □	8:14-25 □	8:26-40 □	9:1-19 □	9:20-43 □	10:1-16 □	10:17-33 □
42	10:34-48 □	11:1-18 □	11:19-30 □	12:1-25 □	13:1-12 □	13:13-43 □	13:44—14:5 □
43	14:6-28 □	15:1-12 □	15:13-34 □	15:35—16:5 □	16:6-18 □	16:19-40 □	17:1-18 □
44	17:19-34 □	18:1-17 □	18:18-28 □	19:1-20 □	19:21-41 □	20:1-12 □	20:13-38 □
45	21:1-14 □	21:15-26 □	21:27-40 □	22:1-21 □	22:22-29 □	22:30—23:11 □	23:12-15 □
46	23:16-30 □	23:31—24:21 □	24:22—25:5 □	25:6-27 □	26:1-13 □	26:14-32 □	27:1-26 □
47	27:27—28:10 □	28:11-22 □	28:23-31 □	Rom. 1:1-2 □	1:3-7 □	1:8-17 □	1:18-25 □
48	1:26—2:10 □	2:11-29 □	3:1-20 □	3:21-31 □	4:1-12 □	4:13-25 □	5:1-11 □
49	5:12-17 □	5:18—6:5 □	6:6-11 □	6:12-23 □	7:1-12 □	7:13-25 □	8:1-2 □
50	8:3-6 □	8:7-13 □	8:14-25 □	8:26-39 □	9:1-18 □	9:19—10:3 □	10:4-15 □
51	10:16—11:10 □	11:11-22 □	11:23-36 □	12:1-3 □	12:4-21 □	13:1-14 □	14:1-12 □
52	14:13-23 □	15:1-13 □	15:14-33 □	16:1-5 □	16:6-24 □	16:25-27 □	1 Cor. 1:1-4 □

Reading Schedule for the Recovery Version of the New Testament with Footnotes

Wk.	Lord's Day	Monday	Tuesday	Wednesday	Thursday	Friday	Saturday
53	1 Cor. 1:5-9 ☐	1:10-17 ☐	1:18-31 ☐	2:1-5 ☐	2:6-10 ☐	2:11-16 ☐	3:1-9 ☐
54	3:10-13 ☐	3:14-23 ☐	4:1-9 ☐	4:10-21 ☐	5:1-13 ☐	6:1-11 ☐	6:12-20 ☐
55	7:1-16 ☐	7:17-24 ☐	7:25-40 ☐	8:1-13 ☐	9:1-15 ☐	9:16-27 ☐	10:1-4 ☐
56	10:5-13 ☐	10:14-33 ☐	11:1-6 ☐	11:7-16 ☐	11:17-26 ☐	11:27-34 ☐	12:1-11 ☐
57	12:12-22 ☐	12:23-31 ☐	13:1-13 ☐	14:1-12 ☐	14:13-25 ☐	14:26-33 ☐	14:34-40 ☐
58	15:1-19 ☐	15:20-28 ☐	15:29-34 ☐	15:35-49 ☐	15:50-58 ☐	16:1-9 ☐	16:10-24 ☐
59	2 Cor. 1:1-4 ☐	1:5-14 ☐	1:15-22 ☐	1:23—2:11 ☐	2:12-17 ☐	3:1-6 ☐	3:7-11 ☐
60	3:12-18 ☐	4:1-6 ☐	4:7-12 ☐	4:13-18 ☐	5:1-8 ☐	5:9-15 ☐	5:16-21 ☐
61	6:1-13 ☐	6:14—7:4 ☐	7:5-16 ☐	8:1-15 ☐	8:16-24 ☐	9:1-15 ☐	10:1-6 ☐
62	10:7-18 ☐	11:1-15 ☐	11:16-33 ☐	12:1-10 ☐	12:11-21 ☐	13:1-10 ☐	13:11-14 ☐
63	Gal. 1:1-5 ☐	1:6-14 ☐	1:15-24 ☐	2:1-13 ☐	2:14-21 ☐	3:1-4 ☐	3:5-14 ☐
64	3:15-22 ☐	3:23-29 ☐	4:1-7 ☐	4:8-20 ☐	4:21-31 ☐	5:1-12 ☐	5:13-21 ☐
65	5:22-26 ☐	6:1-10 ☐	6:11-15 ☐	6:16-18 ☐	Eph. 1:1-3 ☐	1:4-6 ☐	1:7-10 ☐
66	1:11-14 ☐	1:15-18 ☐	1:19-23 ☐	2:1-5 ☐	2:6-10 ☐	2:11-14 ☐	2:15-18 ☐
67	2:19-22 ☐	3:1-7 ☐	3:8-13 ☐	3:14-18 ☐	3:19-21 ☐	4:1-4 ☐	4:5-10 ☐
68	4:11-16 ☐	4:17-24 ☐	4:25-32 ☐	5:1-10 ☐	5:11-21 ☐	5:22-26 ☐	5:27-33 ☐
69	6:1-9 ☐	6:10-14 ☐	6:15-18 ☐	6:19-24 ☐	Phil. 1:1-7 ☐	1:8-18 ☐	1:19-26 ☐
70	1:27—2:4 ☐	2:5-11 ☐	2:12-16 ☐	2:17-30 ☐	3:1-6 ☐	3:7-11 ☐	3:12-16 ☐
71	3:17-21 ☐	4:1-9 ☐	4:10-23 ☐	Col. 1:1-8 ☐	1:9-13 ☐	1:14-23 ☐	1:24-29 ☐
72	2:1-7 ☐	2:8-15 ☐	2:16-23 ☐	3:1-4 ☐	3:5-15 ☐	3:16-25 ☐	4:1-18 ☐
73	1 Thes. 1:1-3 ☐	1:4-10 ☐	2:1-12 ☐	2:13—3:5 ☐	3:6-13 ☐	4:1-10 ☐	4:11—5:11 ☐
74	5:12-28 ☐	2 Thes. 1:1-12 ☐	2:1-17 ☐	3:1-18 ☐	1 Tim. 1:1-2 ☐	1:3-4 ☐	1:5-14 ☐
75	1:15-20 ☐	2:1-7 ☐	2:8-15 ☐	3:1-13 ☐	3:14—4:5 ☐	4:6-16 ☐	5:1-25 ☐
76	6:1-10 ☐	6:11-21 ☐	2 Tim. 1:1-10 ☐	1:11-18 ☐	2:1-15 ☐	2:16-26 ☐	3:1-13 ☐
77	3:14—4:8 ☐	4:9-22 ☐	Titus 1:1-4 ☐	1:5-16 ☐	2:1-15 ☐	3:1-8 ☐	3:9-15 ☐
78	Philem. 1:1-11 ☐	1:12-25 ☐	Heb. 1:1-2 ☐	1:3-5 ☐	1:6-14 ☐	2:1-9 ☐	2:10-18 ☐

Reading Schedule for the Recovery Version of the New Testament with Footnotes

Wk.	Lord's Day		Monday		Tuesday		Wednesday		Thursday		Friday		Saturday	
79	Heb. 3:1-6	☐	3:7-19	☐	4:1-9	☐	4:10-13	☐	4:14-16	☐	5:1-10	☐	5:11—6:3	☐
80	6:4-8	☐	6:9-20	☐	7:1-10	☐	7:11-28	☐	8:1-6	☐	8:7-13	☐	9:1-4	☐
81	9:5-14	☐	9:15-28	☐	10:1-18	☐	10:19-28	☐	10:29-39	☐	11:1-6	☐	11:7-19	☐
82	11:20-31	☐	11:32-40	☐	12:1-2	☐	12:3-13	☐	12:14-17	☐	12:18-26	☐	12:27-29	☐
83	13:1-7	☐	13:8-12	☐	13:13-15	☐	13:16-25	☐	James 1:1-8	☐	1:9-18	☐	1:19-27	☐
84	2:1-13	☐	2:14-26	☐	3:1-18	☐	4:1-10	☐	4:11-17	☐	5:1-12	☐	5:13-20	☐
85	1 Pet. 1:1-2	☐	1:3-4	☐	1:5	☐	1:6-9	☐	1:10-12	☐	1:13-17	☐	1:18-25	☐
86	2:1-3	☐	2:4-8	☐	2:9-17	☐	2:18-25	☐	3:1-13	☐	3:14-22	☐	4:1-6	☐
87	4:7-16	☐	4:17-19	☐	5:1-4	☐	5:5-9	☐	5:10-14	☐	2 Pet. 1:1-2	☐	1:3-4	☐
88	1:5-8	☐	1:9-11	☐	1:12-18	☐	1:19-21	☐	2:1-3	☐	2:4-11	☐	2:12-22	☐
89	3:1-6	☐	3:7-9	☐	3:10-12	☐	3:13-15	☐	3:16	☐	3:17-18	☐	1 John 1:1-2	☐
90	1:3-4	☐	1:5	☐	1:6	☐	1:7	☐	1:8-10	☐	2:1-2	☐	2:3-11	☐
91	2:12-14	☐	2:15-19	☐	2:20-23	☐	2:24-27	☐	2:28-29	☐	3:1-5	☐	3:6-10	☐
92	3:11-18	☐	3:19-24	☐	4:1-6	☐	4:7-11	☐	4:12-15	☐	4:16—5:3	☐	5:4-13	☐
93	5:14-17	☐	5:18-21	☐	2 John 1:1-3	☐	1:4-9	☐	1:10-13	☐	3 John 1:1-6	☐	1:7-14	☐
94	Jude 1:1-4	☐	1:5-10	☐	1:11-19	☐	1:20-25	☐	Rev. 1:1-3	☐	1:4-6	☐	1:7-11	☐
95	1:12-13	☐	1:14-16	☐	1:17-20	☐	2:1-6	☐	2:7	☐	2:8-9	☐	2:10-11	☐
96	2:12-14	☐	2:15-17	☐	2:18-23	☐	2:24-29	☐	3:1-3	☐	3:4-6	☐	3:7-9	☐
97	3:10-13	☐	3:14-18	☐	3:19-22	☐	4:1-5	☐	4:6-7	☐	4:8-11	☐	5:1-6	☐
98	5:7-14	☐	6:1-8	☐	6:9-17	☐	7:1-8	☐	7:9-17	☐	8:1-6	☐	8:7-12	☐
99	8:13—9:11	☐	9:12-21	☐	10:1-4	☐	10:5-11	☐	11:1-4	☐	11:5-14	☐	11:15-19	☐
100	12:1-4	☐	12:5-9	☐	12:10-18	☐	13:1-10	☐	13:11-18	☐	14:1-5	☐	14:6-12	☐
101	14:13-20	☐	15:1-8	☐	16:1-12	☐	16:13-21	☐	17:1-6	☐	17:7-18	☐	18:1-8	☐
102	18:9—19:4	☐	19:5-10	☐	19:11-16	☐	19:17-21	☐	20:1-6	☐	20:7-10	☐	20:11-15	☐
103	21:1	☐	21:2	☐	21:3-8	☐	21:9-13	☐	21:14-18	☐	21:19-21	☐	21:22-27	☐
104	22:1	☐	22:2	☐	22:3-11	☐	22:12-15	☐	22:16-17	☐	22:18-21	☐		

Week 1 — Day 1

Today's verses

1 John
1:1-2

That which was from the beginning, which we have heard, which we have seen with our eyes, which we beheld and our hands handled, concerning the Word of life (and the life was manifested, and we have seen and testify and report to you the eternal life, which was with the Father and was manifested to us).

Date _____

Week 1 — Day 2

Today's verses

Matt.
4:21

...He saw another two brothers, James the *son* of Zebedee and John his brother...mending their nets; and He called them.

1 Cor.
1:10

Now I beseech you, brothers, through the name of our Lord Jesus Christ, that you all speak the same thing and *that* there be no divisions among you, but *that* you be attuned in the same mind and in the same opinion.

Date _____

Week 1 — Day 3

Today's verses

John
1:4

In Him was life, and the life was the light of men.

10:10

The thief does not come except to steal and kill and destroy; I have come that they may have life and may have *it* abundantly.

11:25

...I am the resurrection and the life; he who believes into Me, even if he should die, shall live.

Date _____

Week 1 — Day 4

Today's verses

1 John
5:16

If anyone sees his brother sinning a sin not unto death, he shall ask and he will give life to him, to those sinning not unto death. There is a sin unto death; I do not say that he should make request concerning that.

3:16

In this we know love, that He laid down His life on our behalf, and we ought to lay down our lives on behalf of the brothers.

Date _____

Week 1 — Day 5

Today's verses

1 John
1:3

That which we have seen and heard we report also to you that you also may have fellowship with us, and indeed our fellowship is with the Father and with His Son Jesus Christ.

7

But if we walk in the light as He is in the light, we have fellowship with one another, and the blood of Jesus His Son cleanses us from every sin.

Date _____

Week 1 — Day 6

Today's verses

John
12:24

Truly, truly, I say to you, Unless the grain of wheat falls into the ground and dies, it abides alone; but if it dies, it bears much fruit.

1 Cor.
10:17

Seeing that there is one bread, we who are many are one Body; for we all partake of the one bread.

Date _____

Week 2 — Day 4   Today's verses

John 7:39 But this He said concerning the Spirit, whom those who believed into Him were about to receive; for *the* Spirit was not yet, because Jesus had not yet been glorified.

1 Cor. 15:45 ...The last Adam *became* a life-giving Spirit.

Date

Week 2 — Day 1   Today's verses

John 6:46 Not that anyone has seen the Father, except Him who is from God, He has seen the Father.

7:29 I know Him, because I am from Him, and He sent Me.

1:18 No one has ever seen God; the only begotten Son, who is in the bosom of the Father, He has declared *Him*.

Date

Week 2 — Day 5   Today's verses

Luke 24:26 Was it not necessary for the Christ to suffer these things and enter into His glory?

Phil. 1:19 For I know that for me this will turn out to salvation through your petition and *the* bountiful supply of the Spirit of Jesus Christ.

Date

Week 2 — Day 2   Today's verses

John 1:29 The next day he saw Jesus...and said, Behold, the Lamb of God, who takes away the sin of the world!

19:34 But one of the soldiers pierced His side with a spear, and immediately there came out blood and water.

Date

Week 2 — Day 6   Today's verses

John 16:13 But when He, the Spirit of reality, comes, He will guide you into all the reality; for He will not speak from Himself, but what He hears He will speak; and He will declare to you the things that are coming.

20:22 And when He had said this, He breathed into *them* and said to them, Receive the Holy Spirit.

Date

Week 2 — Day 3   Today's verses

John 15:26 But when the Comforter comes, whom I will send to you from the Father, the Spirit of reality, who proceeds from the Father, He will testify concerning Me.

4:24 God is Spirit, and those who worship Him must worship in spirit and truthfulness.

Date

Week 3 — Day 4   Today's verses

John 11:25   Jesus said..., I am the resurrection and the life; he who believes into Me, even if he should die, shall live.

14:2   In My Father's house are many abodes; if it were not so, I would have told you; for I go to prepare a place for you.

Date _____

Week 3 — Day 5   Today's verses

John 2:19   Jesus answered and said to them, Destroy this temple, and in three days I will raise it up.

21-22   But He spoke of the temple of His body. When therefore He was raised from the dead, His disciples remembered that He had said this, and they believed the Scripture and the word which Jesus had spoken.

Date _____

Week 3 — Day 6   Today's verses

John 1:14   And the Word became flesh and tabernacled among us (and we beheld His glory, glory as of the only Begotten from the Father), full of grace and reality.

14:23   Jesus answered and said..., If anyone loves Me, he will keep My word, and My Father will love him, and We will come to him and make an abode with him.

Date _____

Week 3 — Day 1   Today's verses

John 10:10-11   The thief does not come except to steal and kill and destroy; I have come that they may have life and may have it abundantly. I am the good Shepherd; the good Shepherd lays down His life for the sheep.

15   Even as the Father knows Me and I know the Father; and I lay down My life for the sheep.

Date _____

Week 3 — Day 2   Today's verses

John 10:9   I am the door; if anyone enters through Me, he shall be saved and shall go in and go out and shall find pasture.

Matt. 9:36   And seeing the crowds, He was moved with compassion for them, because they were harassed and cast away like sheep not having a shepherd.

Date _____

Week 3 — Day 3   Today's verses

John 10:16   And I have other sheep, which are not of this fold; I must lead them also, and they shall hear My voice, and there shall be one flock, one Shepherd.

21:16   ...Simon, *son* of John, do you love Me? He said to Him, Yes, Lord, You know that I love You. He said to him, Shepherd My sheep.

Date _____

Week 4 — Day 4 — Today's verses

Rev. And in the midst of the lampstands One
1:13-14 like the Son of Man,…girded about at the breasts with a golden girdle. And His head and hair were as white as wool, as snow; and His eyes were like a flame of fire.

Dan. I watched until thrones were set, and the
7:9 Ancient of Days sat down. His clothing was like white snow, and the hair of His head was like pure wool; His throne was flames of fire, its wheels, burning fire.

Date

Week 4 — Day 5 — Today's verses

Rev. And His feet were like shining bronze, as
1:15-16 having been fired in a furnace; and His voice was like the sound of many waters. And He had in His right hand seven stars…

Dan. …His arms and His feet like the gleam of
10:6 polished bronze, and the sound of His words like the sound of a multitude.

Date

Week 4 — Day 6 — Today's verses

Rev. …Out of His mouth proceeded a sharp
1:16-18 two-edged sword; and His face *shone* as the sun shines in its power. And when I saw Him, I fell at His feet as dead; and He placed His right hand on me, saying, Do not fear; I am the First and the Last and the living One; and I became dead, and behold, I am living forever and ever; and I have the keys of death and of Hades.

Date

Week 4 — Day 1 — Today's verses

Rev. The revelation of Jesus Christ which God
1:1 gave to Him to show to His slaves the things that must quickly take place; and He made *it* known by signs, sending *it* by His angel to His slave John.

2:7 He who has an ear, let him hear what the Spirit says to the churches. To him who overcomes, to him I will give to eat of the tree of life, which is in the Paradise of God.

Date

Week 4 — Day 2 — Today's verses

Rev. Who testified the word of God and the
1:2 testimony of Jesus Christ, *even* all that he saw.

9 I John, your brother and fellow partaker in the tribulation and kingdom and endurance in Jesus, was on the island called Patmos because of the word of God and the testimony of Jesus.

Date

Week 4 — Day 3 — Today's verses

Rev. And in the midst of the lampstands One like
1:13 the Son of Man, clothed with a garment reaching to the feet, and girded about at the breasts with a golden girdle.

Exo. …Every morning when he dresses the
30:7 lamps.…

Eph. For no one ever hated his own flesh, but
5:29 nourishes and cherishes it, even as Christ also the church.

Date

Week 5 — Day 4   Today's verses

Matt. ...The kingdom of the heavens is like
13:33 leaven, which a woman took and hid in three measures of meal until the whole was leavened.

Rev. But I have *something* against you, that you
2:20 tolerate the woman Jezebel, she who calls herself a prophetess and teaches and leads My slaves astray to commit fornication and to eat idol sacrifices.

18:2 ...Fallen, fallen is Babylon the Great!...

Date

Week 5 — Day 1   Today's verses

Heb. Hence also He is able to save to the utter-
7:25 most those who come forward to God through Him, since He lives always to intercede for them.

Rev. ...And out of His mouth proceeded a
1:16 sharp two-edged sword....

2:1 ...These things says He who holds the seven stars in His right hand, He who walks in the midst of the seven golden lampstands.

Date

Week 5 — Day 5   Today's verses

Rev. And He cried with a strong voice, saying,
18:2 Fallen, fallen is Babylon the Great! And she has become a dwelling place of demons and a hold of every unclean spirit and a hold of every unclean and hateful bird.

7 As much as she has glorified herself and lived luxuriously, as much torment and sorrow give to her; for she says in her heart, I sit a queen, and I am not a widow, and I shall by no means see sorrow.

Date

Week 5 — Day 2   Today's verses

Exo. And Aaron...every morning when he dress-
30:7 es the lamps...

27:20 And you shall command the children of Israel to bring to you pure oil of beaten olives for the light, to make the lamps burn continually.

Date

Week 5 — Day 6   Today's verses

Rev. So, because you are lukewarm and nei-
3:16 ther hot nor cold, I am about to spew you out of My mouth.

2:7 He who has an ear, let him hear what the Spirit says to the churches. To him who overcomes, to him I will give to eat of the tree of life, which is in the Paradise of God.

Matt. But the prudent took oil in their vessels
25:4 with their lamps.

Date

Week 5 — Day 3   Today's verses

Rev. I know where you dwell, where Satan's
2:13-15 throne is...But I have a few things against you, that you have some there who hold the teaching of Balaam, who taught Balak to put a stumbling block before the sons of Israel, to eat idol sacrifices and to commit fornication. In the same way you also have some who hold in like manner the teaching of the Nicolaitans.

Date

Week 6 — Day 4

Today's verses

Rev. And I saw as it were a glassy sea mingled
15:2-3 with fire and those who come away victorious from the beast and from his image and from the number of his name standing on the glassy sea, having harps of God. And they sing the song of Moses, the slave of God, and the song of the Lamb, saying, Great and wonderful are Your works, Lord God the Almighty! Righteous and true are Your ways, O King of the nations!

Date _____

Week 6 — Day 5

Today's verses

Rev. ...The marriage of the Lamb has come, and
19:7-8 His wife has made herself ready. And it was given to her that she should be clothed in fine linen, bright *and* clean; for the fine linen is the righteousnesses of the saints.

S. S. Return, return, O Shulammite; return, re-
6:13 turn, that we may gaze at you. Why should you gaze at the Shulammite, as upon the dance of two camps?

Date _____

Week 6 — Day 6

Today's verses

Rev. And the armies which are in heaven fol-
19:14 lowed Him on white horses, dressed in fine linen, white *and* clean.

21:10-11 And he...showed me the holy city, Jerusalem, coming down out of heaven from God, having the glory of God. Her light was like a most precious stone, like a jasper stone, as clear as crystal.

Date _____

Week 6 — Day 1

Today's verses

Rev. ...John, who testified the word of God
1:1-2 and the testimony of Jesus Christ, *even all* that he saw.

11-12 ...What you see write in a scroll and send *it* to the seven churches: to Ephesus and to Smyrna and to Pergamos and to Thyatira and to Sardis and to Philadelphia and to Laodicea. And I turned to see the voice that spoke with me; and when I turned, I saw seven golden lampstands.

Date _____

Week 6 — Day 2

Today's verses

Rev. After these things I saw, and behold, *there*
7:9 *was* a great multitude which no one could number, out of every nation and *all* tribes and peoples and tongues, standing before the throne and before the Lamb, clothed in white robes and palm branches in their hands.

17 ...The Lamb who is in the midst of the throne will shepherd them and guide them to springs of waters of life; and God will wipe away every tear from their eyes.

Date _____

Week 6 — Day 3

Today's verses

Rev. And a great sign was seen in heaven: a
12:1 woman clothed with the sun, and the moon underneath her feet, and on her head a crown of twelve stars.

5 And she brought forth a son, a man-child, who is to shepherd all the nations with an iron rod; and her child was caught up to God and to His throne.

Date _____